First World War
and Army of Occupation
War Diary
France, Belgium and Germany

41 DIVISION
Divisional Troops
Divisional Signal Company
1 May 1916 - 29 November 1917

WO95/2627/1

The Naval & Military Press Ltd
www.nmarchive.com
Published in association with The National Archives

Published by

The Naval & Military Press Ltd

Unit 10 Ridgewood Industrial Park,

Uckfield, East Sussex,

TN22 5QE England

Tel: +44 (0) 1825 749494

www.naval-military-press.com

www.nmarchive.com

This diary has been reprinted in facsimile from the original. Any imperfections are inevitably reproduced and the quality may fall short of modern type and cartographic standards.

© Crown Copyright
Images reproduced by permission of The National Archives, London, England, 2015.

Contents

Document type	Place/Title	Date From	Date To
Heading	WO95/2627/1		
Heading	41 Division Divl Signal Coy 1916 May-1917 Oct To Italy 1917 Nov From Italy 1918 Mar		
War Diary	Aldershot	01/05/1916	01/05/1916
War Diary	Havre	02/05/1916	04/05/1916
War Diary	Merris	05/05/1916	29/05/1916
War Diary	Steenwerck	30/05/1916	02/06/1916
Diagram etc			
Miscellaneous			
War Diary	Steenwerck	03/06/1916	31/07/1916
War Diary	Field	24/06/1916	27/07/1916
Operation(al) Order(s)	41st. Division Order No 20.	02/07/1916	02/07/1916
Miscellaneous	Movement Table in accordance with 41st Division Order No. 20.		
Operation(al) Order(s)	41st Division Order No. 21.	06/07/1916	06/07/1916
Miscellaneous	Amendment To 41st Division Operation Order No 21.	06/07/1916	06/07/1916
Operation(al) Order(s)	41st Division Order No. 22.	08/07/1916	08/07/1916
Operation(al) Order(s)	41st Division Order No. 25.	10/07/1916	10/07/1916
Miscellaneous	Amendment to 41st Division Order No. 23.	12/07/1916	12/07/1916
Operation(al) Order(s)	41st. Division Order No. 24.	13/07/1916	13/07/1916
Miscellaneous	Amendment To 41st. Division Order No. 24.	14/07/1916	14/07/1916
Operation(al) Order(s)	41st Division Order No 25.	16/07/1916	16/07/1916
Miscellaneous	41st Div. G. 254. (68/8).	18/07/1916	18/07/1916
Operation(al) Order(s)	41st Divisional Order No. 26.	18/07/1916	18/07/1916
Operation(al) Order(s)	41st Division Order No. 27.	18/07/1916	18/07/1916
Miscellaneous	Time-Table of Operations.		
Miscellaneous	Amendment to 41st Division Order No. 26.	20/07/1916	20/07/1916
Operation(al) Order(s)	41st Division Order No. 28.	23/07/1916	23/07/1916
Operation(al) Order(s)	41st Division Order No. 29.	24/07/1916	24/07/1916
Miscellaneous	Movement Table to Accompany 41st Division Order No. 29.		
Operation(al) Order(s)	41st Division Order No. 30.	26/07/1916	26/07/1916
Miscellaneous	Movement Table to Accompany 41st Division Order No. 30 of 26-7-16		
Operation(al) Order(s)	41st Division Order No. 31	27/07/1916	27/07/1916
Operation(al) Order(s)	41st Division Order No. 32.	29/07/1916	29/07/1916
War Diary	Steenwerck	01/08/1916	17/08/1916
War Diary	Fletre	18/08/1916	25/08/1916
War Diary	Ailly Le Haut Clocher	25/08/1916	31/08/1916
War Diary		06/08/1916	11/08/1916
Operation(al) Order(s)	41st Division Order No. 33.	05/08/1916	05/08/1916
Operation(al) Order(s)	41st Division Order No. 34.	07/08/1916	07/08/1916
Miscellaneous	Vth Corps.		
Operation(al) Order(s)	41st Division Order No. 35.	15/08/1916	15/08/1916
Miscellaneous	Movement Table to Accompany 41st Div. Order No. 35 of 13-8-16		
Miscellaneous	Explanatory Note to 41st Division Order No. 35.	13/08/1916	13/08/1916
Operation(al) Order(s)	41st Division Order No. 36.	20/08/1916	20/08/1916
Heading	41 Div. Signal Coy. R.E. War Diary September 1916. Vol 5		

War Diary	Ailly Le Haut Clocher	01/09/1916	05/09/1916
War Diary	Buire Sur L'Ancre	06/09/1916	10/09/1916
War Diary	Bellevue Farm	11/09/1916	18/09/1916
War Diary	Ribemont	25/09/1916	30/09/1916
War Diary	Field	22/08/1916	25/09/1916
Operation(al) Order(s)	41st Division Order No. 37.	05/09/1916	05/09/1916
Miscellaneous	March Table to Accompany 41st Divisional Order No. 37		
Operation(al) Order(s)	41st Division Order No. 38.	05/09/1916	05/09/1916
Operation(al) Order(s)	41st Division Order No. 39.	10/09/1916	10/09/1916
Miscellaneous	41st Div. Signal Co.	10/09/1916	10/09/1916
Operation(al) Order(s)	41st Division Order No. 40.	11/09/1916	11/09/1916
Operation(al) Order(s)	41st Division Order No. 44.	14/09/1916	14/09/1916
Operation(al) Order(s)	41st Division Order No. 41.	13/09/1916	13/09/1916
Operation(al) Order(s)	41st Division Order No. 43.	14/09/1916	14/09/1916
Miscellaneous	Diary Of Communications, 15th. Septr. 1916.	16/09/1916	16/09/1916
Miscellaneous	A Form. Messages And Signals.		
Operation(al) Order(s)	41st Division Order No. 45.	17/09/1916	17/09/1916
Miscellaneous			
Miscellaneous	Diary Of Communications, 16-9-16.	17/09/1916	17/09/1916
Miscellaneous	Report On Signal Communications during Offensive Operations 14th-17th Septr 1915.		
Miscellaneous	Diary Of Communications, 17-9-1916.	18/09/1916	18/09/1916
Heading	War Diary 41 Div. Sig. Coy. R.E. October 1916. Vol 6		
War Diary	Ribemont	01/10/1916	03/10/1916
War Diary	Fricourt Chateau	04/10/1916	09/10/1916
War Diary	Buire	11/10/1916	15/10/1916
War Diary	Hallencourt	16/10/1916	19/10/1916
War Diary	Fletre	20/10/1916	23/10/1916
War Diary	Reninghelst	24/10/1916	31/10/1916
War Diary	Field	01/10/1916	24/10/1916
Miscellaneous	Report On 41st. Div. Signal Communications during Offensive Operations October 5th-11th.		
Miscellaneous	Orders Regarding Signal Communications From 4th October, 1916.	03/10/1916	03/10/1916
Diagram etc	Circuit Diagram		
Diagram etc	Communications 21st D.A.		
Miscellaneous	Diary Of Communications. Period-30-9-16 to 7-10-16.	08/10/1916	08/10/1916
Miscellaneous	A	27/10/1916	27/10/1916
Heading	41st. Div. Signal Coy. R.E. War Diary For November 1916. Vol 7		
War Diary	Reninghelst	01/11/1916	29/11/1916
War Diary	Field	07/11/1916	06/12/1916
War Diary	Reninghelst	01/12/1916	28/02/1917
War Diary	Field	28/01/1917	10/02/1917
Heading	War Diary of 41st. Div. Signal Coy R.E. for month of March 1917 Vol XI		
War Diary	Reninghelst	06/03/1917	31/03/1917
War Diary	Reninghelst	01/03/1917	30/04/1917
War Diary		01/04/1917	18/04/1917
War Diary	Reninghelst	04/05/1917	27/05/1917
War Diary	Reninghelst	28/04/1917	19/05/1917
War Diary	Berthen	27/05/1917	28/06/1917
War Diary	Westoutre	22/06/1917	22/06/1917
War Diary	Berthen	30/06/1917	30/06/1917
War Diary		29/06/1917	29/06/1917

Type	Location/Description	From	To
War Diary	Berthen	01/07/1917	25/07/1917
War Diary	Westoutre	25/07/1917	31/07/1917
War Diary	Berthen	03/07/1917	24/07/1917
War Diary	Westoutre	01/08/1917	15/08/1917
War Diary	Berthen	15/08/1917	21/08/1917
War Diary	Wizernes	21/08/1917	27/08/1917
War Diary		26/07/1917	17/08/1917
War Diary		19/07/1917	06/08/1917
War Diary	Wizernes	01/09/1917	14/09/1917
War Diary	Zevecoten	15/09/1917	22/09/1917
War Diary	Zevecoten & Caestre	23/09/1917	23/09/1917
War Diary	Caestre	24/09/1917	25/09/1917
War Diary	La Panne	26/09/1917	30/09/1917
War Diary	In The Field	27/08/1917	25/09/1917
Miscellaneous	41st. Divisional Signal School. Standing Orders.	11/09/1917	11/09/1917
War Diary	La Panne	01/10/1917	06/10/1917
War Diary	St Idesbalde	07/10/1917	28/10/1917
War Diary	St Malo Les Bains	29/10/1917	31/10/1917
Miscellaneous		28/08/1917	31/10/1917
Miscellaneous	122nd Infantry Brigade. 123rd Infantry Brigade. 124th Infantry Brigade. C.R.A. Camp Commandant. "Q". 41st Divl. Signal Coy. Divisional Signal School.	05/10/1917	05/10/1917
War Diary	St Idesbalde	27/10/1917	27/10/1917
War Diary	Malo	31/10/1917	29/11/1917
Operation(al) Order(s)	41st Signal Coy Order No 5	23/11/1917	23/11/1917
Miscellaneous	St Sylvester.	23/11/1917	23/11/1917
Miscellaneous	St Jefferies	23/11/1917	23/11/1917
Operation(al) Order(s)	41st Signal Coy Order No 7.	25/11/1917	25/11/1917
Operation(al) Order(s)	41st Divl Signal Coy Order No. 6	24/11/1917	24/11/1917
Operation(al) Order(s)	41st Signal Coy. Order No. 8	27/11/1917	27/11/1917

MO95/292/1

41 DIVISION

DIVL SIGNAL COY

1916 MAY — 1917 OCT

To ITALY 1917 NOV
FROM   "   1918 MAR

Army Form C. 2118

WAR DIARY
or
INTELLIGENCE SUMMARY

(Erase heading not required.)

41st Divisional Signal Company R.E.

Vol. 1. 2

Place	Date 1916	Hour	Summary of Events and Information	Remarks and references to Appendices
Aldershot	1 May	3.20 pm	H.Q. & No 1 Section entrained	
		5.30 pm	" " entrained Southampton Docks on S.S. African Prince	
HAVRE	2 May	10 am	disembarked Havre & marched to Rest Camp No. 1.	
	3 May	noon	Entrained at Havre	
	4 May	11 am	detrained GODEWAERSVELDE & marched to MERRIS. Division forms part of 2nd Corps, 2nd Army. Telephonic communication with 2nd Corps.	
MERRIS	5 May		Divisional HQ arrive & established in Convent. Communications to all units have been provided for us by 2nd Army Signals. 122 I.B. arrive and are billeted at OUTERSTEENE.	
	6 May		123 I.B. arrive in Strazeele area	
MERRIS	7 May		124 I.B. arrive RENESCURE — telegraphic communication only via BCD and Hazebrouck —	
	8 May		20 N.C.O.s and men sent up to Nieppe to occupy lines etc preparatory to taking over from 9th Division	

WAR DIARY
or
INTELLIGENCE SUMMARY

Army Form C. 2118

Place	Date	Hour	Summary of Events and Information	Remarks and references to Appendices
MERRIS	9 May		122 I.B. Group move to BAILLEUL & area. Communication from Bde. & ready	
			124 I.B. group move to OUTTERSTEENE & area.	
			10 N.C.O.'s from each section go up to 9th Division area to learn lines etc they will eventually take over.	
"	10 May		Nothing to report	
"	11 May		" "	
"	21 May		The situation remains unchanged	
"	27 May morn		41 Div. Artillery relieve the 9th Div' arty. in the line	
"	28 May p.m.		122 I.B. move to TRABST & an Bde in reserve under 9th Div. Send parties to Steenwerck and Nieppe to take over signal offices from 9th D's Signals at 3 am	
STEENWERCK	30 "		Company move. After ychrist and enough personal to run the Ahmad 41 Div at NIEPPE & company to the Ahmad 41 Div at NIEPPE. Rear party came on from Merris after 11am at which hour the official change of Div Hqs. takes place. Very heavy rain & work in the div office all day. Div HQ X manages in first 10 hours which is unusual at a divmove. Now H.E. (turn)	

WAR DIARY or INTELLIGENCE SUMMARY

Army Form C. 2118

Place	Date	Hour	Summary of Events and Information	Remarks and references to Appendices
STEENWERCK	30/5/16	(cont'd)	lines at Div Hq are labelled so that we could locate on the permanent ones. 3 DRLS were very busy. Owing to the difficulty of keeping track of units as they moved, DR2 was hardly back from one delivery before others started with the next. 122 Bde were left sector today.	
"	31/5/16		123 Bde later on right sector tonight. Still a press for DR2 corps for the long part of the day, as still many Bns Telegraph lines to re-establish & rearrange movements on the telephone. Never a new elective line, & never a number of lines and by the evening we were able to light 9 and 9 lighting at around Erkery and the regnl Hqrs. Hundreds of staff and the enemy shovelled half everything settling down nicely. Dr. of I of D, Army D of S.	
"	1/6/16		New scheme for DRLS was on force with many fewer places of call for the DR2 and were local delivery. Result a great speeding up of the whole system. Have taken away the 2 DRs lent to the RA for the more & 3 days are being my tent worked hugely easy to unnecessary orderly work are DRLS. Completed the leading in of the new arm permanent antenna (4 line wire) from YDAR and the Test-Point, to the new Hq for the Bde in rest.	
"	2/6/16		Remains. Incidentally Lt Patrick completed 120 rd of the 4 line write on arduous detachment from his cable section	

WAR DIARY
or
INTELLIGENCE SUMMARY

(Erase heading not required.)

Army Form C. 2118

41st Div. Circuit diagram
MERRIS 5 May /16.

- FRI
- PRADELLES — FSZ
- CAESTRE — FRC, FRG
- STAZEELE — ZDC
- Div Train
- YDA
- BCO
- OUTTERSTEENE — ZLB

WAR DIARY
or
INTELLIGENCE SUMMARY

Army Form C. 2118

Place	Date	Hour	Summary of Events and Information	Remarks and references to Appendices
			The following Casualties occurred during May '16 94902 Dpr Spain J. Died in No 7 Gen Hospital on 23rd from Erysipelas. One Horse was evacuated on the 19th. One O.R arrived from Base Depot on 25th.	

N.D Murphy Lieut Capt
O/C 41 Sig Co, 12 S

Army Form C. 2118

WAR DIARY
or
INTELLIGENCE SUMMARY
(Erase heading not required.)

Instructions regarding War Diaries and Intelligence Summaries are contained in F.S. Regs., Part II. and the Staff Manual respectively. Title Pages will be prepared in manuscript.

Place	Date	Hour	Summary of Events and Information	Remarks and references to Appendices
STEENWERCK	3/6/16		About a dozen shells fell in Nieppe between 2 and 3 am but only a splinter or two fell in our camp — no harm done. 16 Divn artillery were out in two places by 5.9.2 between YDIAR and T.P. but we were through the 3' trenches that nestle the Div we went to the forward trench however it had so over Have been very busy at Nieppe since we little we cleaning up etc. The camp and rectg. huts, also trenches to make the lines and for the men to wash at etc.	
	6/6/16		Having a lot of trouble with the Infantry and artillery signallers who in so many cases know little or nothing about these work. The greatest trouble arose over the SOS line: The Infantry brigade battalions are out all and every day trying to educate their battalion signallers. The want of a properly trained signal officer with each BN is currently felt. Bury at Headquarters working at a scheme for 6 post. have arrived rates, but to our existing encumbrance, and in view of a possible Scheme for L'hauee has been completed and sent out to its staff. All has been most lately. The battalion circuits have now been got out a much more satisfactory condition.	
	10/6/16			

WAR DIARY or INTELLIGENCE SUMMARY

Army Form C. 2118

(Erase heading not required.)

Place	Date	Hour	Summary of Events and Information	Remarks and references to Appendices
STEENWERCK 15/6/16	15/6/16		Received 14, 4 hour draught exchange from 2nd Lupo yesterday. They are not quite so good as the five horses we had with Jackie and Phye. The latter are about fit and are the very best remount. Daylight shoeing came in last night. Still having trouble with the SOS lines in the right sector, mainly owing to the batteries having no conception of maintenance.	
	17/6/16		Our first gas attack was experienced between about 12.15 am and 2.0 am this morning. The Bn got a whiff but most of it came diagonally across from the division on our left. She went on very light and the wind it about 10 miles per hour and several of them are still setting off. The DRs call was very stale. The result was the telephone exchange at YDAR was much delayed. There was a very heavy rush on the wires had at the time of receiving enemy had to war opportunities so the Bn goes up. This has never been done to make the appeal signal, but the horses and mules are anything a good deal better. There was no gun at Dr Hy.	
	19/6/16		2nd Corps move and we come under 5th Corps again. Though 1st Anzac Corps regards supply in most of our requirements. 2nd Lt PATMAN joined the company today from BAR	

WAR DIARY or INTELLIGENCE SUMMARY

Army Form C. 2118

Place	Date	Hour	Summary of Events and Information	Remarks and references to Appendices
Steenwerck	21/6/16		Started to have cable between Guide-Post and S.S.I was installed by Corps instead of by Cable Company. We got 500 men from 123 Bde. They were to finish it by Corps arrangements. We got it finished the night 20/21st. had we not got men for the service we could not have got it done at all. There was a gas alarm on the night and we are doing a scheme beyond me or ours dug outs. The scheme we got out for the service is a ...
We are getting on better with the 6/F. have men as we are able to keep the men on the all. They have finished a track. We have two dug outs attached to help with the service — Lt. LARKIN since 22nd and 2/Lt Henderson since 21st. We have also 5 men from the 47th admin Section who came to us on 28th inst.	
	26/6/16		Working party attached for digging last night unable to come get up to S.S.I as enemy still fire in PLOEGSTEERT WOOD. As they had to work in the open, it was ... they could not up for time to be able to complete work before daylight so a partially dry trench only full all the working party was dismissed. No working parties available today as the ...	
	30/6/16		Division to have a march intensive.	

WAR DIARY
or
INTELLIGENCE SUMMARY

(Erase heading not required.)

Army Form C. 2118

Place	Date	Hour	Summary of Events and Information	Remarks and references to Appendices
	11th June		The following increases of establishment are noted —	
			Authorised under W.O. letter No 121/7926 (S.D.2) dt. 9/5/16.	
			To each cable section — 2 pioneers. Increase of 4 Pnrs.	
			To div. Signal Cy. 4 pioneers — Trained as Telephone teleg. operators.	
	21st June		Authorised under W.O. letter No 121/7926 (S.D.2) dt 17/6/16.	
			Six Officer telegraphists for duty with Trench Wireless Sets.	
			Total increase of establishment under the W.O. letters quoted above = 14 other ranks.	

WAR DIARY or INTELLIGENCE SUMMARY

Army Form C. 2118

The following Casualties occurred during June '16
One N.C.O. transferred to 2nd Army Signal Coy.
One O.R. evacuated to No 7 Cas Clearing Stn Fn 20th
One O.R. evacuated to 1st Canadian Clearing Stn on 26th
One O.R. joined from Base Signal Depot on 1st
Two O.Rs   "   "   "   "   "   "   4th
One O.R.   "   "   "   "   "   "   15th
Five O.R.   "   "   "   "   "   "   18th
Two Horses were evacuated on 1st and 6th
One Horse was shot on the 16th having had off hind leg broken the result of a kick.
Two O.R. joined from Signal Depot Base on May 25th
Six O.R. were sent to 2nd Army Signal School to be trained as "Wireless Operators" on the 6th
Course to last about six weeks —

N.C. Murgatroyd Lieut/R
O.C. 41 Signal Company R.E.

2/7/16

WAR DIARY
INTELLIGENCE SUMMARY

Army Form C. 2118

41st Division Signal Company NZ

Vol 3

Place	Date	Hour	Summary of Events and Information	Remarks and references to Appendices
STEENWERCK	1916 July 2nd July		During yesterday 30/6/16 the artillery bombarded the hostile trenches and cut the line in various places. During the evening 8 craters were cut by gas & smoke — the hostile trenches were raided in three places. Hostile shelling broke the buried (8ft) line to 124 Bde in 8 places at about 11pm.	
	3 July		Have now put the pigeon loft at Pluzzepe on to the buzzer exchange at YDAR and by this means have speeded up the time for proper microppo considerably. Best time taken for a pigeon message sent from Pluzypoort wood to Div HQ. at Steenwerck is now 10 minutes formerly it was 19 minutes.	
	4 July		122 Bde taking over more trenches to day has extended the front of the division. Their HQ. from 10.30pm 4 inst. is at PETITE MUNAVE FM. To connect them to YDAR three cables (telephone pair & sounder) were yesterday laid from a test box at the "Rat Hole" HQ. Division front now extends from R 2f5 — R.D30V6.	

Army Form C. 2118

WAR DIARY
or
INTELLIGENCE SUMMARY
(Erase heading not required.)

Instructions regarding War Diaries and Intelligence Summaries are contained in F.S. Regs., Part II. and the Staff Manual respectively. Title Pages will be prepared in manuscript.

Place.	Date	Hour	Summary of Events and Information	Remarks and references to Appendices
STEENWERCK	5-7 July		Listening to record.	
	6		Op. Order No 21 recd	
	7			
	8 July		2/LtR PATMAN was returned to 2 Army Signal Coy for further training - D.D.M.S. L Army informs me there is no Officer at present available to replace him.	
			Lieut. LARKING & 6 Sprs. who had been lent to this unit temp'ly in cable burying, returned to 1st ANZAC Corps who are leaving this area.	
			2/Lieut. JEFFRIES arrived vice Lt LARKING for temporary attachment for Cable Burying.	
			The Cable burying progresses — in 17 days 6900 yds. have been buried, more than half of this in PLOEGSTEERT WOOD where roots & water have made digging very difficult.	
	11 July		The Officer i/c 110. R. arrive & are temporarily attached in cable burying.	
	12 July		NIEPPE received some shells about 8 km which broke the Souastre line & 12 copt. Pole line was put through on burried route	

1875 Wt. W593/826 1,000,000 4/15 J.B.C. & A. A.D.S.S./Forms/C. 2118.

Place	Date	Hour	Summary of Events and Information	Remarks and references to Appendices
STEEN WERCK	13/7/16		Another B/P. Buried cable route was completed yesterday i.e. CINDER FARM — HILL 63 —	
"	17/7/16.		The telephone switchboard at YPDAR which was a very old pattern, having become very faulty & causing a lot of trouble daily was changed yesterday afternoon. A Span 10 line board & one board of one board sent away to 2nd Army to overhaul. The Old board sent away to 2nd Army to overhaul. The Sounder line to 723 I.B. which runs through the sewers & which having become very earthy has been temporarily replaced by an overhead cable, which the sewer line will be relaid.	
"	22/7/16		The Cable bringing switches daily — we are now getting 200 men in the morning & 200 in the afternoon — they average about 300 yards daily — The General Situation remains unchanged — units occupy the same positions — A good many lines of cavalry have been taken by shell fire lately, but are quickly repaired.	

WAR DIARY or INTELLIGENCE SUMMARY

Army Form C. 2118

Place	Date	Hour	Summary of Events and Information	Remarks and references to Appendices
STEENWERCK	27/1/16		Raids carried out last night have been successful, many German corpses being found in the trenches. The front held by division is again being shelled. The left brigade coming out & going into its old position in the advd. HQ at Cinder Farm & peace HQ at Romarin. Move takes place tomorrow 28 & under.	
	28/1/16		To test alternative means of communication from 10 — 11.30 am today all wires in front of Bde HQ were assumed to be cut. Pigeons, visual & DRs were to be used instead. The time of suspension was too short to effectively test alternative means & it will be tried again. Some messages were sent by visual from & from by pigeon. The quickest message yet received by pigeon service is 7 minutes from a Baynal report centre [?] 3 receipt in this office. NIEPPE was shelled by heavy guns yesterday afternoon, a direct hit in the church was obtained.	
	30/1/16		NIEPPE again shelled at 30th, 9.31.5¹ one shell bursting into the sewers and broke our surrender line to 22 C. Starting on 22/6/16 to Curry Cable 6 ft deep up to & including 31/7/16 a length of 10,200 yds has been completed. About 15,000 men have been employed —	

Army Form C. 2118

WAR DIARY
or
INTELLIGENCE SUMMARY
(Erase heading not required.)

1st / Div: Signal Coy. R.E.

Place	Date	Hour	Summary of Events and Information	Remarks and references to Appendices
Field	2/6		The following Canadian reserves during the month.	
	28/6		96637 Spr. Watson 2 was evacuated to 1st Canadian Cas. Clearing Sta.	
	6/7		5 Other Ranks (Reinforcements) from Base Signal Depot	
	7/7		2/Lt R. Palmer left to join 2nd Army Signal Coy.	
	8/7		2 Other Ranks (Reinfs) from Base Signal Depot	
	"		1 " was evacuated to No. 2 Canadian Clearing Sta.	
	13/7		94895 Sgt. Sutton E. wounded to Corporal at his own request.	
	14/7		94895 Cpl Sutton E. left to join 2nd Army Signal Coy.	
	15/7		93687 Cpl Sheward H. and 27152 Cpl. Chappell W. joined from 2nd Army Sig Coy.	
	16/7		3 OR. joined from Base Sig Depot – 1 Reinf. 2 to complete arms establishment.	
	17/7		37344 Cpl. Musgrave T. evacuated to 2d Canadian Clearing Sta.	
	19/7		Cpl Chappell appcld. acting Sergt.	
	25/7		93757 Dr. Stephens R. left for Base Signal Depot en route for England for ship building work.	
	27/7			

Walmsley Lieut
OC. 41 Div Signal Coy RE

SECRET.   COPY NO...11...

41ST. DIVISION ORDER NO 20.

July 2nd, 1916.

1.   41st Division order No 19 of 30th June 1916 is cancelled.

2.   The 41st Division will extend its front Northward and take over the trenches from ANTONS FARM to the RIVER DOUVE.

3.   On completion of the move the front will be divided in sectors with dispositions as follows:-

RIGHT SECTOR.- 123rd Inf Bde.
    From the R.LYS to Trench 111 (inclusive).
    Brigade H.Q. at PONT DE NIEPPE.
    Support Battalions at LE BIZET and SOYER FARM.

CENTRE SECTOR.- 124th Inf Bde.
    From Trench 112 (incl) to Trench 124 (incl).
    Brigade H.Q. - PAPOT.
    1 Battalion (Support) CRESLOW.
    1 Battalion (Divisional Reserve) PAPOT.

LEFT SECTOR.- 122nd Inf Bde.
    From Trench 125 inclusive to R.DOUVE.
    Brigade H.Q. - PETITE MUNQUE FARM.
    1 Battalion (Support) PIGGERIES.
    1 Battalion (Divisional Reserve) GRANDE MUNQUE FARM and PLOEGSTEERT WOOD (T.24.b.6.8.).

4.   The Dividing Lines between the above sectors will be,

(a) Between Right and Centre Sectors. Junction Trench 111 and 112 - Junction GORDON AVENUE and NORFOLK AVENUE - BORDER AVENUE (to both sectors) - MAISON 75 (to Centre Sector).

(b) Between Left and Centre Sectors. Junction Trench 112 and 113 - Junction TORONTO AVENUE and ST YVES AVENUE - TORONTO AVENUE - MUDLANE (both to Left Sector).

5.   Infantry Moves in connection with the above will be carried out as under.

(a) Local re-adjustments of the front between the RIVER LYS and ANTONS FARM will be carried out under arrangements to be made between Brigades concerned. All moves to be completed by 12 noon, July 5th.

(b) The 122nd Inf Bde will relieve the 2nd Australian Inf Bde (attached 24th Divn) on the front ANTONS FARM - R.DOUVE, in accordance with attached Table. Details to be arranged between Brigades concerned.

6.   The 41st Div Artillery will cover the front for defence purposes from the R.LYS to ANTONS FARM and will deal with retaliation and bombardment behind German front line from U.15.a.4.8. to LA PETITE DOUVE FARM.

/ The S.O.S.

The S.O.S. along that line being dealt with by 24th Divnl Artillery who will be relieved by Artillery from 1st ANZAC on night 5/6th.

7. The areas allotted to Field Coys R.E. for work will be as follows:-
   <u>233rd Field Coy R.E.</u> From Trenches 132 to 128 (both incl.) and area in Rear.
   <u>228th Field Coy R.E.</u> Trenches 127 - 121 (both incl.) and area in Rear.
   <u>237th Field Coy R.E.</u> Trenches 120 to 111 and area in Rear.
   All work in Right Sector will be carried out by the Infantry. The C.R.E. will detail one officer for attachment to that Brigade to assist.

8. Each Brigade will have its Machine Gun Company for the defence of its Sector. Brig.-Generals Commanding will arrange their dispositions and report same to Divisional Headquarters.
   On completion of move the 10th Motor Machine Gun Bty will be withdrawn into Divisional Reserve at NIEPPE.

9. Tramways are allotted to Sectors as under.
   HIGHLAND RAILWAY to Right Sector.
   N.British and C.P.R. Right Branch to Centre Sector.
   C.P.R. Left Branch) to Left Sector.
   HYDE PARK Railway)

10. The command and responsibility for the defence of the front ANTONS FARM - R.DOUVE will pass to G.O.C. 122nd Inf Bde on completion of the Infantry reliefs on July 4/5th.

11. The 41st Division will assume command of the II Corps front (between RIVERS DOUVE and LYS) from 10 p.m. July 3/4th.

12. Completion of each move and relief will be reported by telegram to Divisional Headquarters.

13. Acknowledge.

H.H.Wilson
Major, G.S.

Copy No 1 - File.
"   " 2 - War Diary.
"   " 3 - "Q".
"   " 4 - C.R.A.
"   " 5 - C.R.E.
"   " 6 - 122nd Inf Bde.
"   " 7 - 123rd Inf Bde.
"   " 8 - 124th Inf Bde.
"   " 9 - 19th Bn Middx Regt.
"   " 10 - A.D.M.S.
"   " 11 - 41st Div Signal Coy.
"   " 12 - Divnl Train.
"   " 13 - New Zealand Divn.
"   " 14 - 24th Division.
"   " 15 - V Corps.
"   " 16 - 10th M.M.G. Bty.
"   " 17 - II Corps H.A.
"   " 18 - Spare.

MOVEMENT TABLE in accordance with 41st DIVISION ORDER No. 20.

Date.	Unit.	From.	To	Remarks.
Night July 3/4.	Advanced Parties, Machine Guns, Lewis Guns & Trench Mortars, 122nd Infantry Bde.	41st Div. Area.	Trenches S. of R. DOUVE.	On relief, Machine Guns &c. 2nd Aust. Bde move to I ANZAC Area.
July 4.	1 Battalion, 122nd Inf. Bde.	41st Div. Area.	GRANDE MUNQUE and PLOEGSTEERT WOOD, T 24 b 6.8.	On relief, one Battalion 2nd Aust. Bde moves to I ANZAC Area.
Night July 4/5.	2 Battalions, 122nd Inf. Bde.	GRANDE MUNQUE and 41st Div. Area.	Trenches S. of R. DOUVE.	On relief, one Battn, 2nd Aust. Bde moves to GRANDE MUNQUE, and one Battn to I ANZAC Area. Bde H.Q. to change with Infantry relief.
Night July 5/6.	1 Battalion, 122nd Inf. Bde.	41st Div. Area.	GRANDE MUNQUE and PLOEGSTEERT WOOD, T 24 b 6.8.	To relieve 1 Battn, 2nd Aust. Bde, which moves to I ANZAC Area.

SECRET.   Copy No. 11

41st DIVISION ORDER No. 21.

6-7-16.

1.-   Minor enterprises will be carried out by the 123rd and 124th Inf. Bdes in co-operation with the 41st Divl Artillery against the enemy's trenches, as follows:-

Sat.   (By 123rd Inf. Bde against trenches at C 4 a 7.6.
8th July   (" 124th   "   "   "   "   " U 15 d 9.4,
            (

Monday,
10th July   By 124th Inf. Bde against trenches at U 22 c 3.3½

2.-   All arrangements for artillery action will be made between G.O's C. Infantry Brigades concerned and the C.R.A.

3.-   Working parties will be suspended between the hours of 11 p.m. and 2 a.m. on those nights.

4.-   The ZERO hour will be communicated to all concerned by Special D.R. on the evening of each operation.

5.-   Acknowledge.

                                                B L Anley
                                                  Lt Col.
                                                    G.S.

                Copy No. 1 - File.
                  "   "   2 - War Diary.
                  "   "   3 - "Q"
                  "   "   4 - C.R.A.
                  "   "   5 - C.R.E.
                  "   "   6 - 122nd Inf. Bde.
                  "   "   7 - 123rd   "   "
                  "   "   8 - 124th   "   "
                  "   "   9 - 19th Middx (Pioneers).
                  "   " 10 - A.D.M.S.
                  "   " 11 - 41st Divl Signal Coy.
                  "   " 12 - 41st Divl Train.
                  "   " 13 - New Zealand Div.
                  "   " 14 - 2nd Australian Div.
                  "   " 15 - Vth Corps.
                  "   " 16 - Second Army.
                  "   " 17 - 10th Motor M. G. Battery.
                  "   " 18 - II Corps Heavy Arty.
                  "   " 19 - IX Corps.
                  "   " 20 - 171st Tunnelling Coy.
                  "   " 21 - 1st Australian Tunnelling Coy.
                  "   " 22 - Spare.

SECRET.

<u>SECRET and URGENT.</u>　　　　　　　　　　　Copy No......11......

<u>AMENDMENT TO 41ST DIVISION OPERATION ORDER NO 21.</u>

　　　　　　　　　　　　　　　　　　　July 8th 1916.

1.　　The Minor Enterprise detailed in 41st Division Order No 21 of 6/7/16 to be carried out by 124th Infantry Bde at U 15 d 9.4. on July 8th will be postponed until night July 9/10th owing to move of 2nd Australian Division.

2.　　The other enterprises will hold good.

3.　　Acknowledge.

　　　　　　　　　　　　　　　　　　　A.M.Wilson.
　　　　　　　　　　　　　　　　　　　Major, G.S.

```
Copy No  1.  - File.
  "   "  2.  - War Diary.
  "   "  3.  - "Q".
  "   "  4.  - C.R.A.
  "   "  5.  - C.R.E.
  "   "  6.  - 122nd Inf Bde.
  "   "  7.  - 123rd Inf Bde.
  "   "  8.  - 124th Inf Bde.
  "   "  9.  - 19th Bn Middx R.
  "   " 10.  - A.D.M.S.
  "   " 11.  - 41st Div Signal Coy.
  "   " 12.  - Divnl Train.
  "   " 13.  - New Zealand Divn.
  "   " 14.  - 2nd Australian Divn.
  "   " 15.  - V Corps.
  "   " 16.  - II Army.
  "   " 17.  - 10th M.M.G. Bty.
  "   " 18.  - II Corps H.A..
  "   " 19.  - IX Corps.
  "   " 20.  - 171st Tunnelling Coy R.E.
  "   " 21.  - 1st Australian Tunnelling Coy.
  "   " 22.  - Spare.
```

SECRET.

Copy No. ......

41st Division Order No.22.

8th July 1916.

1. Provided the wind is favourable (e.g. from W. to S.S.W.) a surprise gas attack will be carried out by personnel of M Coy, 3rd Batt. Special Brigade R.E. at 2.a.m. 13th inst from trench 124, trenches 127, 128, and southern half of trench 129.

2. The bays of the above named trenches which contain cylinders to be temporarily cleared of infantry during the discharge of gas. Any sentry posts left in bays not containing cylinders to wear gas helmets.

3. Smoke will also be discharged by the personnel M Coy, Special Brigade R.E. from the following trenches at the same hour:-

    North half of trench 123.
    North half of trench 124
    Trenches   125, 126
    South half of trench 130

4. Troops in trenches 123, 125, 126, & 130 will take "gas alert" precautions.

5. No artillery, M.G. or rifle fire will be employed in connection with the gas attack.

6. The gas discharge will cease at 2.20.a.m, at which hour troops will re-occupy the trenches temporarily vacated by them.

7. Acknowledge.

B.d. Anley
Lt.Colonel. G.S.

Copies issued at 10.0. a.m. to :-

1. File.
2. War Diary.
3. "Q".
4. C. R. A.
5. C. R. E.
6. 122nd Infy Bde.
7. 123rd Infy Bde.
8. 124th Infy Bde.
9. 13th Middlesex Regt.
10. A. D. M. S.
11. 41st Div. Signal Coy.
12. New Zealand Division.
13. 24th. Division.
14. Second Army.
15. 15th M.M.G. Battery.
16. II Corps H.A.
17. 171st Tunnelling Coy.
18. 1st Australian Tunnelling Coy.
19. M. Co. 3rd Bn Spec Bde R.E.

SECRET.   Copy No. 11

41st Division Order No. 23.

July 10th 1916.

1. Minor operations will be carried out by Infantry Brigades in co-operation with the 41st Divisional Artillery against the enemy's trenches as follows :-

   Night July 12/13th.

   Minor Enterprise by 122nd Infantry Brigade against trenches at U 15 a 7½ 6¼.

   Minor Enterprise by 123rd Infantry Brigade against trenches at C 4 d 1 4½.

   To take place simultaneously by mutual arrangement between Brigadiers concerned.

   2.a.m. Gas discharge from trenches 124, 127, 128, and part of 129 as per 41st Div. Order No.22. of July 8th 1916.

   July 13th.

   12.30.p.m. Smoke discharge by 124th Infantry Bde on front of trenches 112-124 accompanied by bombardment of enemy's front and support lines with shrapnel.

   Night July 14/15th.

   Minor Enterprise by 124th Infantry Brigade against hostile trenches N. of FACTORY FARM.

2. All arrangements for artillery action will be made between General Officers Commanding Infantry Brigades concerned and the C.R.A.

3. Working parties will be suspended on those nights between the hours of 11.p.m. and 2.a.m. (3.a.m. on night 12/13th.)

4. The Zero hour will be communicated to all concerned by special D.R. on the evening of each operation.

5. The result of each enterprise will be reported by PRIORITY Telegram to Divisional Headquarters followed by a detailed report in writing.

6. Acknowledge.

                                                Major. G.S.

P.T.O.

Copy No.	1.	to	File.
" "	2.	"	War Diary.
" "	3.	"	" Q ".
" "	4.	"	C. R. A.
" "	5.	"	C. R. E.
" "	6.	"	122nd Infantry Bde.
" "	7.	"	123rd " "
" "	8.	"	124th " "
" "	9.	"	19th Middlesex Regt.
" "	10.	"	A.D.M.S.
" "	11.	"	41st Div. Sig. Coy.
" "	12.	"	New Zealand Division.
" "	13.	"	24th. Division.
" "	14.	"	Second Army.
" "	15.	"	10th M.M.G.Batty.
" "	16.	"	II Corps H.A.
" "	17.	"	171st Tunnelling Coy.
" "	18.	"	1st Australian Tunnelling Coy.
" "	19.	"	M. Coy. 3rd Batt.Special Bde R.E.
" "	20.	"	Spare.

SECRET & URGENT.   Copy No. 11

AMENDMENT to 41st DIVISION ORDER No. 23.

                                                              12-7-16.

1.-   The minor enterprise detailed in 41st Division Order No. 23 of 8-7-16, to be carried out by 123rd Inf. Bde against trenches at C 4 d 1 4½ on night July 12th/13th, will now take place on night July 13th/14th.

2.-   The enterprise by 122nd Inf. Bde as therein detailed will take place on night July 12th/13th.

3.-   The enterprise by 124th Inf. Bde on night July 14th/15th, will now be carried out on night July 13th/14th.

4.-   General Officers Commanding 123rd and 124th Inf. Bdes will arrange to synchronize by mutual arrangement, the zero time for the enterprises.

5.-   Acknowledge.

                                                   [signature] Wilson
                                                              Major, G.S.

        Copy No. 1 - File.
         "   "   2 - War Diary.
         "   "   3 - "Q"
         "   "   4 - C.R.A.
         "   "   5 - C.R.E.
         "   "   6 - 122nd Inf. Bde.
         "   "   7 - 123rd   "   "
         "   "   8 - 124th   "   "
         "   "   9 - 19th Middx (Pioneers).
         "   " 10 - A.D.M.S.
         "   " 11 - 41st Divl Signal Coy.
         "   " 12 - New Zealand Div.
         "   " 13 - 24th Div.
         "   " 14 - Second Army.
         "   " 15 - 10th Motor M. G. Battery.
         "   " 16 - II Corps H.A.
         "   " 17 - 171st Tunnelling Coy, R.E.
         "   " 18 - 1st Aust. Tunnelling Coy,
         "   " 19 - "M" Coy, 3rd Bn, Special Bde, R.E.
         "   " 20 - Spare.

                                                   ackd [signature]

SECRET.   COPY NO. 11

41ST. DIVISION ORDER NO. 24.

July 13th, 1916.

1. The operations for July 13th, 14th and 15th as detailed in 41st Division Order No 23 of 10/7/16 and the amendment thereto are cancelled.

2. Minor operations will be carried out by Infantry Brigades in co-operation with the 41st Divnl Artillery against the enemy trenches as follows:-

   Night July 13/14th.
   10-30 p.m. Dummy raid and artillery bombardment on hostile trenches at C 4 d 1.4½.
   2-0 a.m.   GAS discharge from trenches 124, 127, 128 and part of 129 as per 41st Division Order No 22 of 8/7/16.

   July 14th. Smoke discharge by 124th Inf Bde on front of trenches 112 - 124 accompanied by bombardment of enemy's front and support lines with shrapnel.

   Night July 14/15th.
   Minor enterprise by 124th Infantry Bde against hostile trenches North of FACTORY FARM.

3. All Arrangements for artillery will be made between G.O.C's, Infantry Brigades concerned and the C.R.A.

4. Working parties will be suspended after 1 a.m. July 14th and on night July 14/15th at the discretion of Sector Commanders.

5. The ZERO hour will be communicated to all concerned by special D.R. on the evening of each operation.

6. The result of each enterprise will be reported by PRIORITY telegram to Divisional H.Q. followed by a detailed account in writing.

7. Acknowledge.

                                                     H.M.Wilson
                                                     Major, G.S.

Copy No 1. - File.   Copy No 17. - 171st Tunnlg
  "   " 2. - War Diary.   Coy R.E.
  "   " 3. - "Q".   "   " 18. - 1st Aust.
  "   " 4. - C.R.A.   Tunnlg Coy.
  "   " 5. - C.R.E.   "   " 19. - "M" Coy. 3rd
  "   " 6. - 122nd Inf Bde.   Bn. Special
  "   " 7. - 123rd Inf Bde.   Bde R.E.
  "   " 8. - 124th Inf Bde.   "   " 20. - Spare.
  "   " 9. - 19th Middx (Pioneers).
  "   " 10. - A.D.M.S.
  "   " 11. - 41st Div Signal Coy.
  "   " 12. - New Zealand Div.
  "   " 13. - 24th Div.
  "   " 14. - Second Army.
  "   " 15. - 10th M.MG Bty.
  "   " 16. - II Corps H.A.

SECRET.

COPY NO. 11

AMENDMENT TO 41ST. DIVISION ORDER NO. 24.

July 14th 1918.

1. The minor enterprise by 124th Infantry Brigade against the hostile trenches North of FACTORY FARM will take place on the night July 15/16th.
   Zero hour will be notified to all concerned.

2. Acknowledge.

                                                H.M. Wilson
                                                   Major, G.S.

```
Copy No.  1. - File.
  "    "  2. - War Diary.
  "    "  3. - "Q".
  "    "  4. - C. R. A.
  "    "  5. - C. R. E.
  "    "  6. - 122nd Infy Bde.
  "    "  7. - 123rd Infy Bde.
  "    "  8. - 124th Infy Bde.
  "    "  9. - 19th Middx (Pioneers).
  "    " 10. - A.D.M.S.
  "    " 11. - 41st Div Signal Coy.
  "    " 12. - New Zealand Div.
  "    " 13. - 24th Div.
  "    " 14. - Second Army.
  "    " 15. - 10th H.F.G.Bty.
  "    " 16. - II Corps R.A.
  "    " 17. - 171st Tunnelling Coy, R.E.
  "    " 18. - 1st Aust. Tunnelling Coy.
  "    " 19. - "F" Coy, 3rd Bn, Special Bde, R.E.
  "    " 20. - Spare.
```

SECRET.   COPY NO. 13

41ST DIVISION ORDER NO 25.

In the Field,
16/7/16.

1.- The following will be the programme for minor operations for the week ending 22nd instant.

	Time.	
Sunday 16th inst.	Morning.	Wire cutting.
	9.35 p.m. to 11.5 p.m.	Rafale fire against WARNETON, PONT ROUGE and LES ECLUSES.
Monday 17th inst.	Morning & Afternoon.	Wire cutting and engage hostile batteries.
Tuesday 18th inst.	9.15 p.m. to 11.15 p.m.	Artillery fire against hostile roads and communications.
Wednesday 19th inst.	Morning.	Wire cutting.
	Night.	Carrying parties - nothing to be done to provoke hostile retaliation.
Thursday 20th inst.	Morning.	Wire cutting.
	Between 12 midnight & 3 a.m.	Surprise gas attack with smoke discharge.
Friday 21st inst.	Morning.	Wire cutting and registration.
	5.30 p.m.	Smoke discharge on front of 123rd Inf Bde, with shrapnel fire against hostile front and support trenches.
	10.15 p.m. to 10.30 p.m.	Dummy raids at U 15 a 8.7. and U 22 c 3.4.
Saturday 22nd inst.	Morning.	Wire cutting.
	Night.	Simultaneous raids by one coy. from 124th Inf Bde and one coy. from 123rd Inf Bde after preliminary bombardment. Zero hour to be notified later.

2.- Acknowledge.

[signature]

Lt.-Colonel, G.S.

P.T.O

Distribution.

Copy No	1	-	Second Army.
" "	2	-	V Corps.
" "	3	-	II Anzac.
" "	4	-	24th Division.
" "	5	-	New Zealand Division.
" "	6	-	C.R.A.
" "	7	-	122nd Infantry Bde.
" "	8	-	123rd Infantry Bde.
" "	9	-	124th Infantry Bde.
" "	10	-	C.R.E.
" "	11	-	19th Middx R.
" "	12	-	A.D.M.S.
" "	13	-	41st Div Signal Coy.
" "	14	-	II Corps H.A.
" "	15	-	171st Tunnelling Coy. R.E.
" "	16	-	1st Australian Tunnelling Coy.
" "	17	-	M. Coy., 3rd Bn, Special Bde, R.E.
" "	18	-	"Q".
" "	19	-	File.
" "	20	-	War Diary.
" "	21	-	Spare.

S E C R E T.   41st Div.
                O. 254.
                (68/8).

~~Second Army.~~
Vth Corps.
II Anzac.
24th Division.
New Zealand Division.
C.R.A.
122nd Infantry Brigade.
123rd Infantry Brigade.
124th Infantry Brigade.
C.R.E.
19th Middx R.
~~A.D.M.S.~~
41st Div Signal Coy.
~~II Corps H.W.~~
171st Tunnelling Coy. R.E.
1st Australian Tunnelling Coy.
N Coy. 3rd Bn. Special Bde. R.E.
"Q".
File.
~~War Diary.~~

Reference 41st Division Order No. 25 dated 16/7/16., please note that Artillery action shown therein for the next three days will be suspended owing to shortage of ammunition.

18/7/1916.

Lt. Colonel, G.S.
for G.O.C. 41st Division.

S E C R E T.   Copy No. 13.

41st Divisional Order No.26.

18th July 1916.

1. Provided the wind is favourable (W. to S.W.) a surprise Gas Attack will be carried out by the Personnel of "M" Coy. 3rd Batt. Special Bde. R.E. on the night July 20/21. from Trenches 93, 96, 97, 98, 99, 100, 101 and 102.

2. The bays of the above named Trenches which contain cylinders will be temporarily cleared of Infantry during the discharge of Gas. Any Sentry Posts left in Bays not containing cylinders will wear GAS HELMETS.

3. Smoke will be discharged by the Personnel "M" Coy. 3rd Batt. Special Bde. R.E. simultaneously with the Gas from the following trenches :-
Trenches 92, 94, 95, 103, 104 & 105.

4. Troops in the Front system of Trenches, between trenches 91 (inclusive) and 106 (inclusive) will take Gas Alert precautions.

5. No Artillery, Machine Gun or Rifle fire will be employed in connection with the Gas Attack.

6. The ZERO hour for the attack will be between hours of 12 midnight and 3.a.m. on night 20/21 July, the actual hour being decided on by O.C. "M" 3rd Batt. Special Bde. R.E. in consultation with G.O.C. 123rd Infantry Brigade so as to suit weather conditions.
O.C. "M" Coy. 3rd Batt. Special Bde. R.E. will be responsible for notifying by code (attached) all concerned, including Divisional Headquarters of the ZERO hour.

7. The trenches cleared will be re-occupied at 0.30. mins.

8. Acknowledge.

Major. G.S.

Copy No. 1. - 2nd Army.   Copy No.11. - 19th Middlesex Regt.
"   " 2. - V Corps.   "   " 12. - A. D. M. S.
"   " 3. - II Anzac Corps.   "   " 13. - 41st Div. Sig. Coy.
"   " 4. - 24th Division.   "   " 14. - II Corps H.A.
"   " 5. - New Zealand Div.   "   " 15. - 171st Tunnelling Coy.
"   " 6. - C. R. A.   "   " 16. - 1st Australian Tun.Coy.
"   " 7. - 122nd Inf Bde.   "   " 17. - "M" Coy. Special Bde.R.E.
"   " 8. - 123rd Inf Bde.   "   " 18. - " Q ".
"   " 9. - 124th Inf Bde.   "   " 19. - File.
"   " 10. - C. R. E.   "   " 20. - War Diary.
                                       "   " 21. - Spare.

Code to accompany 41st Division Order No.28.

```
ZERO.    12 M.N.     Code.    Henry I.
         12.15.a.m.           Henry II.
         12.30.a.m.           Henry III.
         12.45.a.m.           Henry IV.
         1.0. a.m.            Charles I.
         1.15.a.m.            Charles II.
         1.30.a.m.            Charles III.
         1.45.a.m.            Charles IV.
         2.0. a.m.            James I.
         2.15.a.m.            James II.
         2.30.a.m.            James III.
         2.45.a.m.            James IV.
         3.0. a.m.            William I.
```

SECRET.   Copy No. 14

                    41st DIVISION ORDER No. 27.

Ref. Maps: Trench Maps, 1/10,000,   In the Field.
           Sheets 28 S.W.4 and 36 N.W.2.   18-7-16.

INTENTION.   1.- In order to inflict considerable losses on the enemy,
             prevent him withdrawing troops from our front, capture
             prisoners, and do as much damage as possible, a combined
             raid by one company, 123rd Inf. Bde, and one company, 124th
             Inf. Bde, will be carried out on a date to be notified later,
             in accordance with the attached Time Table.

ARTILLERY.   2.- The above combined raid will be prepared and supported
             by the Divisional Artillery, supplemented by a Group of
             Heavy Artillery. Brig.-Generals Commanding 123rd and 124th
             Inf. Bdes will also arrange for the co-operation of Stokes
             Guns, and for covering fire by rifles and machine guns on
             the flanks of the localities to be attacked.

OBJECTIVES. 3.- (a) One company, 123rd Inf. Bde, will attack the
             hostile front and support line trenches in the RED HOUSE
             locality, in accordance with the detailed scheme drawn up
             by Brig.-General Commanding 123rd Inf. Bde.
                 (b) One company, 124th Inf. Bde, will attack the
             hostile front line trenches from U 28 a 3½ 8 to U 22 c 4 2
             and the support trenches behind them, in accordance with
             the detailed scheme drawn up by Brig.-General Commanding
             124th Inf. Bde.
                 Both the companies will be accompanied by demolition
             parties provided by the R.E.

ZERO HOUR.   4.- The time of zero hour will be notified from Div. H.Q.

WATCHES.   5.- Watches will be synchronized at 5 p.m. on the date of
             attack, Divisional Time being given to all concerned,
             including II Corps Heavy Artillery.

REPORTS.   6.- The result of each raid to be reported by PRIORITY
             telegram to Div. H.Q., followed by a detailed account in
             writing.

             7.- Acknowledge.

                                                      B.L. Anley
                                                      Lt.-Colonel, G.S.

Copies issued at   to:-
   Copy No. 1 - Second Army.   Copy No. 11 - 19th Middlesex Regt.
    "   " 2 - Vth Corps.   "   " 12 - C.R.E.
    "   " 3 - II ANZAC CORPS.   "   " 13.- A.D.M.S.
    "   " 4 - 24th Division.   "   " 14 - 41st Div. Sig. Coy.
    "   " 5 - New Zealand Div.   "   " 15 - 171st Tunnelling Coy.
    "   " 6 - II Corps H.A.   "   " 16 - 1st Australian Tun.Coy.
    "   " 7 - C.R.A.   "   " 17 - "M" Coy. 3rd Batt.
    "   " 8 - 122nd Inf. Bde.   Special Bde. R.E.
    "   " 9 - 123rd   "   "   "   " 18 - "Q".
    "   " 10 - 124th   "   "   "   " 19 - File.
                                      "   " 20 - War Diary.
                                      "   " 21 - Spare.

TIME-TABLE of OPERATIONS.

Date.	Hour.	Operations.
Y Day.	All day.	Wire cutting by Divl. Artillery & T.Ms, and registration by Heavy Artillery.
Z Day.	1 hour before Zero.	Bombardment of points of attack by Heavy Artillery, Divl. Artillery, T.Ms. & Stokes Guns in accordance with detailed programmes drawn up by C.R.A. & Inf. Bdes. Counter battery work by Heavy Artillery.
"	0.0 (Zero hour)	Bombardment lifts from hostile front line, and barrages formed round localities to be attacked. Bombardment to continue on enemy support trenches. Attacking Companies advance from their positions of assembly against the hostile trenches.
"	0.10.	Bombardment lifts from hostile support trenches. Barrages to continue until O.C., Enterprise in each sector notifies Artillery that the party has returned to our trenches.

SECRET.   Copy No. 13.

Amendment to 41st Division Order No. 26.
                    ---------------   20th July, 1916.

1.   Owing to the wind being unfavourable on night
     20th/21st inst. the gas discharge arranged for that night
     has been postponed.

2.   The operations arranged for Friday 21st inst. and
     Saturday 22nd inst. are also postponed.

3.   Acknowledge.

                                           B.L. Anley
                                           Lieut-Col. G.S.

     Copies issued at   to :-

     Copy No. 1 - 2nd Army.
      "   " 2 - V Corps.
      "   " 3 - II Anzac Corps.
      "   " 4 - 20th Division.
      "   " 5 - New Zealand Div.
      "   " 6 - C.R.A.
      "   " 7 - 122nd Inf.Bde.
      "   " 8 - 123rd Inf.Bde.
      "   " 9 - 124th Inf.Bde.
      "   " 10 - C.R.E.
      "   " 11 - 19th Middx.Regt.
      "   " 12 - A.D.M.S.
      "   " 13 - 41st Div.Sig.Coy.
      "   " 14 - II Corps H.A.
      "   " 15 - 171st Tunnelling Coy.
      "   " 16 - 1st Australian Tun.Coy.
      "   " 17 - "M" Coy.3rd Bn. Spec.Bde R.E.
      "   " 18 - "Q".
      "   " 19 - File.
      "   " 20 - War Diary.
      "   " 21 - Spare.

SECRET.   Copy No. 14

41st DIVISION ORDER No. 28.

23-7-16.

INTENTION. 1.— Reference 41st Division Order No. 27 dated 18-7-16, the combined raids therein mentioned will be carried out on Wednesday night, 26th inst. The Company, 124th Inf. Bde, will attack the enemy trenches between U 22 c 4 2 and U 22 c 3 4 and the support line in rear.

ZERO HOUR. 2.— Zero hour will be 12 midnight, 26th inst.

3.— Acknowledge.

B.L. Anley
Lt.-Colonel, G.S.

Issued at 8.5 p.m., to:—

    Copy No. 1 - Second Army.
      "   " 2 - Vth Corps.
      "   " 3 - II ANZAC.
      "   " 4 - 36th Div.
      "   " 5 - New Zealand Div.
      "   " 6 - II Corps H.A.
      "   " 7 - C.R.A.
      "   " 8 - 122nd Inf. Bde.
      "   " 9 - 123rd   "   "
      "   " 10 - 124th   "   "
      "   " 11 - 19th Middx R.
      "   " 12 - C.R.E.
      "   " 13 - A.D.M.S.
      "   " 14 - 41st Divl Signal Coy.
      "   " 15 - 171st Tunnelling Coy, R.E.
      "   " 16 - 1st Australian Tunnelling Coy.
      "   " 17 - "M" Coy, 3rd Bn, Special Bde, R.E.
      "   " 18 - "Q"
      "   " 19 - File.
      "   " 20 - War Diary.
      "   " 21 - Spare.

SECRET.   Copy No.... 13 ...

41st DIVISION ORDER No. 29.

24/7/16.

1. The 41st Division will be relieved on the front RIVER DOUVE to Trench 127 (inclusive) by the 36th Division, V Corps, and will take over the left Sector, New Zealand Division, II Anzac Corps.

2. The 122nd Infantry Brigade and 233rd Field Company R.E. will be relieved on the front RIVER DOUVE – Trench 127 (inclusive) by the 109th Infantry Brigade and a Field Company R.E., 36th Division. The 122nd Infantry Brigade and 2 sections 228th Field Company R.E. will relieve the 2nd New Zealand Brigade and a Field Company R.E., New Zealand Division, on the front RIVER LYS – Trench 76 (inclusive), in accordance with attached Time Table. All details of relief to be arranged between Brigades concerned. Arrangements for relief of Field Companies R.E. to be made between C.R.E's 36th, New Zealand and 41st Divisions.

3. Relief of Advanced Dressing Stations will be made between A.D.M.S. 41st Division and A.D.M.S. 36th and New Zealand Divisions.

4. All movements will be by Platoons at 200 yards distance and precautions will be taken against observation by hostile aircraft.

5. The 124th Infantry Brigade will extend its left and take over the front up to Trench 126 inclusive. The movement to be completed by 12 midnight July 27/28th.

6. The boundary for defence between 36th Division and 41st Division will be as follows :-

    From junction of trenches 126 and 127 to PROWSE POINT (U 14 d 9 9) – to POOLES COTTAGES (U 14 d 2 3) – to OXFORD FORT (U 19 b 3 2) (all inclusive to 36th Division with exception of left branch of C.P.Railway which is retained by 41st Division) – thence in a straight line to the moat South of GRANDE MUNQUE FARM at T 24 d 5 5 – thence west to road junction at T 22 d 4 2 and G.H.Q. 2nd line at T 22 c 4 2 – to G.H.Q. 3rd line at S.24 central.

7. The 41st Divisional Artillery will continue to cover the front of the Sector taken over by the 109th Infantry Brigade. The Left Group covering the Sector from Trench 127 to RIVER DOUVE will come under the tactical control of G.O.C. 36th Division at 12 noon the 28th inst.
   The New Zealand Divisional Artillery will continue to cover the front of the Sector taken over by the 122nd Infantry Brigade.

8. The tactical control of the troops of the 41st Division South of the RIVER LYS will be exercised by the G.O.C. New Zealand Division, but they will continue to be administered by the 41st Division.

9. The Command of the Sector from Trench 127 to RIVER DOUVE will pass to the Brigadier-General Commanding 109th Infantry Brigade, on the night 28/29th inst on completion of Infantry reliefs in the front line.

The Command of the front of 2nd New Zealand Brigade will pass to the Brigadier-General Commanding 122nd Infantry Brigade, on the night 29/30th inst on completion of the relief.

10. All trench stores will be handed over to relieving units.

A record of all stores handed and taken over will be kept by 122nd Infantry Brigade.

11. Defence schemes, Log Books, Intelligence Reports, Tables of Work in hand and proposed, and all documents which may be of value to relieving units will be handed over.

Similar documents etc will be taken over from the 2nd New Zealand Brigade.

122nd Infantry Brigade will keep a record of all documents etc handed and taken over.

12. The completion of all moves and reliefs will be reported by telegram to Divisional Headquarters.

13. Acknowledge.

H.M.Wilson
Major. G.S.

Issued at 10.0 p.m., to :-

Copy No. 1. - Second Army.
"   "   2. - Vth Corps.
"   "   3. - II Anzac Corps.
"   "   4. - 36th Division.
"   "   5. - New Zealand Division.
"   "   6. - C. R. A.
"   "   7. - 122nd Infantry Brigade.
"   "   8. - 123rd   do.   do.
"   "   9. - 124th   do.   do.
"   " 10. - C. R. E.
"   " 11. - 19th Middlesex Regiment.
"   " 12. - A. D. M. S.
"   " 13. - 41st Div.Signal Company.
"   " 14. - II Corps H.A.
"   " 15. - 171st Tunnelling Company.
"   " 16. - 1st Australian Tunnelling Coy.
"   " 17. - "M" Coy.3rd Battn.Special Bde. R.E.
"   " 18. - " Q ".
"   " 19. - File
"   " 20. - War Diary.
"   " 21. - Spare.

MOVEMENT TABLE to accompany 41st DIVISION ORDER No. 29.

Date.	Unit.	From.	To.	In relief of.	Position of unit after relief.	Remarks.
Night July 27/28	Adv. Parties, M.G's, 109th I. Bde (36th Div.)	KORTEPYP. Area.	Trenches, Left Sector, 41st Div.	M.G's & T.M's 122nd Inf. Bde.	NIEPPE.	2 Sections, 228th F'd Co. R.E. to move to Left Sector, N.Z.Div., under arrangement to be made between C.R.E.'s concerned. Remainder of Coy to remain for work in Centre Sector under arrangements to be made by C.R.E.
	2 Bns, 109th Inf.Bde. (36th Div.)	KORTEPYP Area.	GRANDE MUNQUE & G.H.Q. line.	2 Bns, 122nd Inf. Bde.	Bivouac in B 10 a & c.	T.M's of 122nd Inf. Bde will be withdrawn from the Sector without relief.
Night July 28/29	Adv. Parties, M.G's, T.M's, 122nd Inf.Bde.	NIEPPE and B 10 a & c.	Trenches, Left Sector, N.Z.Div.	M.G's & T.M's 2nd N.Z.Bde.	New Zealand Area.	Relief of 233rd F'd Co. R.E. by a F'd Co R.E. 36th Div. - on completion, 233rd F'd Co. R.E. will remain in present billets.
	2 Bns, 122nd I. Bde.	B 10 a & c.	HOUPLINES & Subsidiary Line Left Sector, N.Z.Div.	2 Bns, 2nd N.Z. Bde.	New Zealand Area.	Relief of Advanced Dressing Stations to be arranged between A.D.M.S's concerned.
	2 Bns, 109 I. B.(36th Div.)	KORTEPYP Area.	GRANDE MUNQUE & G.H.Q. Line.	2 Bns, 122 I. Bde.	109 I. Trenches.	) Command to pass on completion of) relief.
	2 Bns, 109 I. Bde. (36th Div.)	GRANDE MUNQUE & G.H.Q. Line.	Trenches, Left Sector, 41st Div.	2 Bns, 122 I. Bde.	Bivouac in B 10 a & c	) Bde H.Q. to move to PAPOT.
Night July 29/30	2 Bns, 122 I. Bde.	HOUPLINES and Subsidiary Line	HOUPLINES and Subsidiary Line Bde.	2 Bns, 122 I. Bde.	2 Bns, 122 I. Trenches.	)
	2 Bns, 122 I. Bde.	HOUPLINES and Subsidiary Line	Trenches, Left Sector, N.Z.Div.	2 Bns, 2nd N. Z. Bde.	N.Z. Area.	) Command to pass on completion of relief.

SECRET.   Copy No. 13.

41st DIVISION ORDER No. 30.

26/7/16.

1.   41st Division Order No.29 of 24/7/16 is cancelled.

2.   The 122nd Infantry Brigade and 233rd Field Company R.E. will be relieved on the front Trench 128 inclusive to RIVER DOUVE by 109th Infantry Brigade and a Field Company R.E., 36th Division, and will move into Divisional Reserve in accordance with attached table.

3.   123rd and 124th Infantry Brigades will readjust their front and dispositions as under :-

    <u>123rd Infantry Brigade</u>. From trenches 90 - 102 both inclusive with 2 Battalions in the Front Line and 2 Battalions in Reserve at LE BIZET and ARMENTIERES.

    <u>124th Infantry Brigade</u>. From trenches 103 - 127 both inclusive with 4 Battalions in Front Line. Relief of Support and Reserve Battalions by Battalions of 122nd Inf Bde will be carried out as per attached table.
All details will be arranged between Brigades concerned.
The Move to be complete by 12 noon 28th instant.

4.   On Completion of Relief, the Divisional Front will be divided into Sectors for purposes of defence as follows :-

    <u>Right Sector</u>. Trenches 90 - 102 both inclusive to 123rd Infantry Brigade, with 2 Battalions in Brigade Reserve.

    <u>Centre Sector</u>. Trenches 103 - 120 (both inclusive) to 124th Infantry Brigade with Sector Reserve — Battalion of Reserve Brigade in SOYER FARM.

    <u>Left Sector</u>. Trenches 121 - 127 (both inclusive) to 122nd Infantry Brigade with Sector Reserve — Battalion of Reserve Brigade in CRESLOW.

    <u>Divisional Reserve</u>.
2 Battalions, Reserve Brigade, at PAPOT and RUE DU SAC.

5.   On completion of relief, Field Companies, R.E. will come under their affiliated Brigades; all details of move being arranged by C.R.E. direct with C.R.E. 36th Div. and Brigadier Generals Commanding Infantry Brigades.

6.-   Relief and readjustment of Advanced Dressing Stations will be made between A.D.M.S. 41st Div. and A.D.M.S. 36th Div.

7.   The 41st Divl Artillery will continue to cover the front of the Sector taken over by the 109th Inf. Bde. The Left Group, covering the Sector from Trench 128 to R. DOUVE, will come under the tactical control of the G.O.C. 36th Div. at 12 noon, 28th inst.

8.- The command of the Sector from Trench 128 to R. DOUVE will pass to the Brig.-General Commanding 109th Inf. Bde on the night 28th/29th inst. on the completion of infantry reliefs in the front line. Command of Sectors on the 41st Divl Front will pass on completion of readjustment.

9.- The boundary for defence between the 36th Div. and the 41st Div. will be as follows:-
Junction, trenches 127-128 - along HYDE PARK RAILWAY (to 36th Div.) - HYDE PARK CORNER - MOAT S. of GRANDE MUNQUE FARM at T 24 d 5 5 - thence West to road junction at T 22 d 4 2 and G.H.Q. 2nd Line at T 22 c 4 2 to G.H.Q. 3rd Line at S 24 central.

See ndr No 31

10.- All movements will be by platoons at 200 yards distance and precautions will be taken against observation by hostile aircraft.

11.- All trench stores will be handed over to relieving units. A record of all stores, handed and taken over, will be kept by Brigades.

12.- Defence Schemes, Log Books, Intelligence Reports, Tables of work in hand and proposed, and all documents which may be of value to relieving units will be handed over. Brigades will keep a record of all documents etc. handed over.

13.- The completion of all moves and reliefs will be reported by telegram to Divisional Headquarters.

14.- Acknowledge.

Major, G.S.

Copies issued at   p.m. as under.

```
Copy No.  1 - Second Army.
 "   "    2 - Vth Corps.
 "   "    3 - II ANZAC Corps.
 "   "    4 - 36th Div.
 "   "    5 - New Zealand Div.
 "   "    6 - C.R.A.
 "   "    7 - 122nd Inf. Bde.
 "   "    8 - 123rd   "     "
 "   "    9 - 124th   "     "
 "   "   10 - C.R.E.
 "   "   11 - 19th Middx R.
 "   "   12 - A.D.M.S.
 "   "   13 - 41st Divl Signal Coy, R.E.
 "   "   14 - II Corps H. A.
 "   "   15 - 171st Tunnelling Co. R.E.
 "   "   16 - 1st Australian Tunnelling Co.
 "   "   17 - "H" Coy, 5rd Bn, Special Bde, R.E.
 "   "   18 - "Q".
 "   "   19 - File.
 "   "   20 - War Diary.
 "   "   21 - Spare.
```

MOVEMENT TABLE to accompany 41st DIVISION ORDER No. 30 of 26-7-16.

Date.	Unit.	From.	To.	In relief of -	Position of unit after relief.	Remarks.
Night July 27/28	Adv. Parties, M.G's, 109th Inf. Bde.	KORTEPYP Area.	Trenches, Left Sector, 41st Div.	M.G's & T.M's 122nd Inf. Bde	RUE DU SAC.	T.M's of 122nd Inf. Bde will be withdrawn without relief.
	2 Bns, 109th Inf. Bde.	KORTEPYP Area.	GRANDE MUNQUE & G.H.Q. Line.	2 Bns, 122nd Inf. Bde.	1 Bn, SOYER FM. 1 Bn, ORESLOW.	In relief of 1 Bn, 123rd Inf. Bde to ARMENTIERES. In relief of 1 Bn, 124th Inf. Bde to trenches.
Night July 28/29	2 Bns, 109th Inf. Bde.	KORTEPYP Area.	Trenches, Left Sector, 41st Div.	2 Bns, 122nd Inf. Bde.	1 Bn, PAPOT. 1 Bn, RUE DU SAC.	In relief of 1 Bn, 124th Inf. Bde to trenches. To Billets now occupied by transport, which will be cleared under arrangements to be made by A & Q, 41st Div.
	Bde H.Q. 109th Inf. Bde.	BAILLEUL.	PETITE MUNQUE.	Bde H.Q.; 122nd Inf. Bde.	PAPOT	In relief of H.Q. 124th Inf. Bde. to LONDON SUPPORT FARM.

SECRET.   Copy No. 13

41st DIVISION ORDER No. 31.

27/7/16.

1. The 41st Division will be attached temporarily to Vth Corps from 12 noon 27/7/16.

2. The Boundary for defence between 36th Division and 41st Division as detailed in Para 9. of 41st Division Order No.30. of 26/7/16 is altered as follows :-

From the junction of Trenches 127 and 128 (U 14 b 10 5) - U 14 d 3 8 - U 14 c 4 3 - road junction U 20 a 2 9 - U 19 b 3 8 (inclusive) - road junction U 19 c 1 9 - T 24 d 5 5 - T 29 b 3 8 - via road to T 22 d 4 2 (inclusive) - G.H.Q. 2nd Line at T 22 c 3 4 - G.H.Q. 3rd line at S.24.central.

3. Acknowledge.

[signature]
Major. G.S.

Copy No. 1. - Second Army.
" " 2. - Vth Corps.
" " 3. - II Anzac Corps.
" " 4. - 36th Division.
" " 5. - New Zealand Division.
" " 6. - C. R. A.
" " 7. - 122nd Infantry Brigade.
" " 8. - 123rd Infantry Brigade.
" " 9. - 124th Infantry Brigade.
" " 10. - C. R. E.
" " 11. - 19th Middlesex Regiment.
" " 12. - A. D. M. S.
" " 13. - 41st Div. Signal Company.
" " 14. - II Corps H.A.
" " 15. - 171st Tunnelling Company.
" " 16. - 1st Australian Tunnelling Coy.
" " 17. - "M" Coy.3rd Bn.Special Bde. R.E.
" " 18. - "Q".
" " 19. - File.
" " 20. - War Diary.
" " 21. - Spare.

SECRET.   Copy No. 14

                    41st DIVISION ORDER No. 32.

                                                           29-7-16.

1.-   The 122nd Inf. Bde will relieve the 124th Inf. Bde in
the Centre and Left Sectors on Thursday, 3rd August. Relief
to be completed by 11-59 p.m. on that date.

2.-   All details of relief, including relief of the Light
Trench Mortar Batteries and Machine Gun Companies in the
Centre and Left Sectors, will be arranged direct between the
Brigades concerned.

3.-   Command to pass on completion of relief, which will be
reported to Div. H.Q. by telegram.

4.-   The H.Q. 124th Inf. Bde will move to its new Headquarters
at B 10 a 4 5 on relief. H.Q. 122nd Inf. Bde will remain at
PAPOT.

5.-   Acknowledge.

                                                B d Auley
                                                Lt.-Colonel, G.S.
Issued at   p.m.

                Copy No. 1 - Vth Corps.
                 "   " 2 - 36th Div.
                 "   " 3 - New Zealand Div.
                 "   " 4 - II Corps H.A.
                 "   " 5 - Vth Corps H.A.
                 "   " 6 - "Q".
                 "   " 7 - C.R.A.
                 "   " 8 - C.R.E.
                 "   " 9 - 122nd Inf. Bde.
                 "   " 10 - 123rd   "   "
                 "   " 11 - 124th   "   "
                 "   " 12 - 19th Middx R.
                 "   " 13 - A.D.M.S.
                 "   " 14 - 41st Divl Signal Coy.
                 "   " 15 - 171st Tunnelling Coy, R.E.
                 "   " 16 - 1st Australian Tunnelling Coy.
                 "   " 17 - File.
                 "   " 18 - War Diary.
                 "   " 19 - Spare.
                 "   " 20 - "M" Coy, 3rd Bn, Special Bde, R.E.

                                Ack'd

Army Form C. 2118

41st Division Signal Coy R.E., WAR DIARY or INTELLIGENCE SUMMARY

Vol 4

(Erase heading not required.)

Instructions regarding War Diaries and Intelligence Summaries are contained in F.S. Regs., Part II. and the Staff Manual respectively. Title Pages will be prepared in manuscript.

Place	Date	Hour	Summary of Events and Information	Remarks and references to Appendices
STEENWERCK	1 Aug.		400 men daily now supplied by the Brigade in rest. These are split up into three parties under Capt. Enodale, Sip. 122 Bde. & Sip. 124 Bde. Capt. Enodale's party is digging between Battery positions & group communications. The 2 parties are digging from Advn. Bde. Report centres up to the front line.	
	3 Aug.		122 Inf. Bde. relieve 124 Inf. Bde. in left & centre sectors.	
	5 Aug.		102 shells fell in huippe between 7.30 pm & 11.30 pm - believed only 3 casualties - (1 man killed & 2 wounded) most of them fell about the Church which is about 300 yards from our camp. No damage or casualties in camp.	
	6 Aug.		Sunday - no working parties. day was observed as second anniversary of the beginning of the war.	
	9 Aug.		124 Inf. Bde. relieve 122 Inf. Bde. in centre & left sectors. MDMS 91st Corps visited Bde- Offices & inspected all the new buried routes.	
	18 Aug.		The O.C. Signal Company visited the SOMME area, returning same day.	

Army Form C. 2118

WAR DIARY
or
INTELLIGENCE SUMMARY
(Erase heading not required.)

Instructions regarding War Diaries and Intelligence Summaries are contained in F. S. Regs., Part II. and the Staff Manual respectively. Title Pages will be prepared in manuscript.

Place	Date	Hour	Summary of Events and Information	Remarks and references to Appendices
STEENWERCK	15 Aug	10 am	The 122 Inf Bde relieved by 70th Bde 23rd Div. 122 I. Bde move to RMBoT	
	16 Aug	9 am	Major stiles O. i/c Sigs. 23 Div. came over & went round Offices with view to taking over. 122. I. B. move to METEREN.	
	17 Aug	9 am	122 I.B. move to THIEUSHOOK. They are in telegraphic communication through 23 Div.	
		6 pm	41 Divn. Closed at STEENWERCK and opened at FLETRE. Same hour.	
FLETRE	18 Aug	11 am	124 I.B. move to METEREN	
		7.40 pm	123 I.B. " " MONT DES CATS.	
	25 Aug	11 am	On nights 19-20 and 20-21 41 Div Arty were relieved by 23rd div Arty. 41 Div communicating lines as follows. Sounder superimposed on ringing telephone pair to ECO - 2LB antzec. Split pair & 1 line sounder, 1 line telephone (to 2LD) (owing to lack of transformers). Telephone pair to CRA at Eecke also dead phone circuits to GOC - 9 staff - Q staff - OC sigs - DADOS. On 23rd - 24th 41 Div entrains for 10 Corps rest area (4th Army). Div Hq. lrns at FHy FLETRE at 2 pm on 24th and opens at AILLY LE HAUT CLOCHER.	

1875 Wt. W593/826 1,000,000 4/15 J.B.C. & A. A.D.S.S./Forms/C. 2118.

Army Form C. 2118

WAR DIARY
or
INTELLIGENCE SUMMARY
(Erase heading not required.)

Place	Date	Hour	Summary of Events and Information	Remarks and references to Appendices
AILLY LE HAUT CLOCHER	Aug 25	11 am	Only wires found here were one pair to ICO at LONG, French permanent wires estimated each end and one used from YDA to ZLC at GOREN FLOS	
	Aug 26		Visual communication now established to all three Brigades - to ZLB via a transmitting station. To ZLC direct to a point about 3/4 m distant then by cycle orderly. To ZLD through one of their battalion HQs. The station at Div HQ established in the Church steeple. Stations are kept open between the following hours 9 am – 1 pm 2.15 – 4.30 pm 5.30 pm – 7.30 pm 9.0 pm – 10.15 pm.	
	Aug 28		Mr Patrick with cable det. built a metallic pair of cerrui airline from BRUCAMPS – 122 hy Bde HQ, joining in to French permanent lines at the former place.	
	Aug 30		Mr Patrick with cable det. built metallic pair in cerrui airline poles from BELLANCOURT – CHATEAU BOIS DE L'ABBEY (124 I.B. HQ) The 3 hy Bdes are now connected to Div HQ each with metallic pairs extended from the French lines by cerrui airline – the French lines are in a bad state and want repairing & clearing everywhere. Several faults (contacts) have appeared in the recent wet and windy weather.	

WAR DIARY
or
INTELLIGENCE SUMMARY

(Erase heading not required.)

Army Form C. 2118

Place	Date	Hour	Summary of Events and Information	Remarks and references to Appendices
AILLY LE HAUT CLOCHER.	31 Aug		Owing to very little work in the Office, Sounder circuits are not being used to Poules. Work being sent over the telephone. Local telephone circuit to HQrs which was built with enamelled wire again is contact. This about the 3rd time the circuit has been faulty — decided to replace by cable tomorrow + not to try enamelled wire again.	

M Mawrthunderhoof
Capt
O.C. 4.1 Div. Signal Cy R.E.
31/8/16.

Army Form C. 2118

WAR DIARY
or
INTELLIGENCE SUMMARY
(Erase heading not required.)

Instructions regarding War Diaries and Intelligence Summaries are contained in F.S. Regs., Part II. and the Staff Manual respectively. Title Pages will be prepared in manuscript.

Place	Date	Hour	Summary of Events and Information	Remarks and references to Appendices
			Casualties during Month of August 1916	
	6/8/16		3 Pioneers and 1 Brigade Section were remustered as "Field drivers" from 97 2 Drivers of the Territorial Force (Yeoman Mounted) arrived from Base Depôt as reinforcements. A.G's Office Base No 3377 dated 14-5-16 authorises their remaining so attached only.	
	7/8/16		1 D.R. evacuated to No 2 Casualty Clearing Station.	
	8/8/16		Car Driver (A.S.C.) evacuated to No 8 Casualty Clearing Stn. Car Driver (A.S.C.) joined as reinforcement from 21/ Div. Supply Col.	
	11/8/16		Two Remts were drawn from Remounts during the month to replace Veterinary Evacuations.	

M.W. Kempthorne
Capt.
O.C. 11 Reynal Cy. R.E.

SECRET.　　　　　　　　　　　　　　　　　　　　　　Copy No. 13

41ST DIVISION ORDER NO. 33.

5th August 1916.

1. The 124th Infantry Brigade will relieve the 122nd Infantry Brigade in the Centre and Left Sectors on Wednesday 9th inst. Relief to be completed by 11.59 p.m. on that date.

2. All details of relief, including reliefs of the Light Trench Mortar batteries and Machine Gun Companies in the Centre and Left Sectors, will be arranged direct between the Brigades concerned.

3. Command to pass on completion of relief which will be reported by telegram to Divisional Headquarters as follows :- D.O. No.33 complied with.

4. Headquarters, 124th Infantry Brigade will remain at LONDON SUPPORT FARM pending completion of the new Headquarters at B 10 a 4.5.

5. Acknowledge.

B L Anley
Lt.Colonel. G.S.

Issued at　　　　p.m.

Copy No			
"	"	1.	V Corps.
"	"	2.	36th Division.
"	"	3.	New Zealand Division.
"	"	4.	V Corps H.A.
"	"	5.	" Q ".
"	"	6.	C. R. A.
"	"	7.	C. R. E.
"	"	8.	122nd Infantry Bde.
"	"	9.	123rd Infantry Bde.
"	"	10.	124th Infantry Bde.
"	"	11.	19th Middlesex Regt.
"	"	12.	A. D. M. S.
"	"	13.	41st Div.Signal Coy.
"	"	14.	171st Tunnelling Coy.
"	"	15.	1st Australian Tunnelling Coy.
"	"	16.	File.
"	"	17.	War Diary.
"	"	18.	Spare.
"	"	19.	"M" Coy. 3rd Bn.Special Bde. R.E.

SECRET.   Copy No. 13

41st DIVISION ORDER No. 34.

7-8-16.

1.- The following minor operations, with the object of inflicting loss on the enemy, will be carried out during the week ending 12th instant.

Night,   ) 10-30 p.m. to 1-0 a.m. - Artillery fire
8th/9th Aug.   ) against hostile roads and communications.

Night,   ) Smoke discharge on front of 124th Inf. Bde
11th/12th Aug.   ) (Trenches 103 - 127) with shrapnel fire
                    against hostile front and support trenches.
                    All details to be arranged between 124th
                    Inf. Bde and Centre Group, 41st Divl Artillery
                    Zero hour will be notified to all concerned.

2.- Acknowledge.

                                                    [signed]
                                                    Major, G.S.

                Copy No. 1 - Vth Corps.
                   "   " 2 - 36th Div.
                   "   " 3 - New Zealand Div.
                   "   " 4 - Vth Corps H.A.
                   "   " 5 - "Q"
                   "   " 6 - C.R.A.
                   "   " 7 - C.R.E.
                   "   " 8 - 122nd Inf. Bde.
                   "   " 9 - 123rd   "   "
                   "   " 10 - 124th   "   "
                   "   " 11 - 19th Middx R. (Pioneers).
                   "   " 12 - A.D.M.S.
                   "   " 13 - 41st Divl Signal Coy.
                   "   " 14 - 171st Tunnelling Co. R.E.
                   "   " 15 - 1st Australian Tunnelling Co.
                   "   " 16 - "M" Coy, 3rd Bn, Special Bde, R.E.
                   "   " 17 - File.
                   "   " 18 - War Diary.
                   "   " 19 - Spare.

S E C R E T.

41st Div.
G. 279.
(68/10)

Vth Corps.
36th Division.
New Zealand Division.
Vth Corps H.A.
C. R. A.
C. R. E.
122nd Infantry Brigade.
123rd Infantry Brigade.
124th Infantry Brigade.
19th Middlesex Regiment.
41st Div. Signal Coy.
171st Tunnelling Coy.
1st Australian Tunnelling Coy.
"M" Coy. 3rd Bn. Special Bde. R.E.

With reference to 41st Division Order No. 34 of 7/8/16.

1. The ZERO hour for the smoke discharge on night of 11/12th August will be 10 p.m.

2. Acknowledge.

Major. G.S.

10/8/16.

SECRET.   Copy No. 15

41ST DIVISION ORDER NO. 35.

13th August 1916.

1. The 41st Division will be relieved by 23rd Division and will move into the Fifth Corps Reserve Area.

2. Reliefs (with the exception of the Divisional Artillery) will be carried out in accordance with attached Movement Table, and will be completed by 12 noon, 18th inst.
   All details of relief will be arranged between Formations, Units and departments of the 23rd and 41st Divisions direct.

3. The 23rd Division Artillery will relieve the 41st Division Artillery on the nights 19/20th and 20th/21st August. Relief to be completed by 12 noon 21st inst, by which hour the 41st Division Artillery will be clear of the 23rd Division area.
   All arrangements for the above will be made between C.R.A's 23rd and 41st Divisions.

4. The completion of the relief by each formation, Unit etc. will be reported by telegraph to Divisional Headquarters.

5. All movements East of PONT D'ACHELLES will be by Platoons, and East of BAILLEUL by companies, at 200 yards distance.

6. All trench stores will be handed over to relieving Units in accordance with instructions issued by "Q" 41st Division.

7. Stokes and Medium Trench Mortars will be brought out of trenches on relief of Trench Mortar Batteries.
   Heavy Trench Mortars will remain in position, and will be handed over.

8. Defence Schemes, Log Books, Intelligence Reports, Tables of Work on hand and proposed, Local Orders, and all documents which may be of value to relieving Units will be handed over.

9. The G.O.C. 23rd Division will assume command of the 41st Division Front at 6 p.m. August 17th. Commands of Sectors will pass on completion of the Infantry Reliefs in the Front Line.

10. The 41st Division Report Centre will close at STEENWERCK at 6 p.m. 17th instant and will open at FLETRE at the same hour.

11. Acknowledge.

A.M.Wilson
Major. G.S.

Issued at 6 AM

```
Copy No.  1.  -  Fifth Corps.
 "   "   2.  -  36th Division.
 "   "   3.  -  New Zealand Division.
 "   "   4.  -  Fifth Corps H.A.
 "   "   5.  -  23rd Division. "G".
 "   "   6.  -  23rd Division. "Q".
 "   "   7.  -  " Q ".
 "   "   8.  -  C. R. A.
 "   "   9.  -  C. R. E.
 "   "  10.  -  122nd Infantry Brigade.
 "   "  11.  -  123rd Infantry Brigade.
 "   "  12.  -  124th Infantry Brigade.
 "   "  13.  -  19th Middlesex Regt. (Pioneers).
 "   "  14.  -  A. D. M. S.
 "   "  15.  -  41st Div. Signal Coy.
 "   "  16.  -  171st Tunnelling Coy. R.E.
 "   "  17.  -  1st Australian Tunnelling Coy.
 "   "  18.  -  "M" Coy. 3rd Bn. Special Bde. R.E.
 "   "  19.  -  File.
 "   "  20.  -  War Diary.
 "   "  21.  -  Spare.
 "   "  22.  -  Spare.
 "   "  23.  -  Spare.
```

M O V E M E N T   T A B L E   to accompany 41st Div. Order No. 35 of 13-8-16.

DATE.	UNIT.	FROM.	TO.	IN RELIEF OF.	TO.	REMARKS.
A. INFANTRY.						
Aug. 14th.	"X" Bde, 23rd Div.	Vth Corps Res. Area.	STEENWERCK Area.	-	-	"X" Bde H.Q. to STEENWERCK.
Aug. 15th.	M.G.Coys & Lt T.M.Batteries 23rd.Div.	Reserve Area.	M.G.Coy & T.M. Transport Lines 41st Div.	-	-	Positions - 122nd I. Bde. B 13 b 39. 123rd " " B 13 d 9 1. 124th " " B 1 c 25.
	"X" Bde, 23rd Div.	STEENWERCK Area.	PAPOT (2 Bns); CRESLOW, SOYER.	122nd Inf. Bde.	LA CRECHE Area.	"X" Bde H.Q. to ROMARIN. 122nd I. Bde H.Q. to RABOT.
	"Y" Bde, 23rd Div.	Reserve Area.	STEENWERCK Area.	"X" Bde, 23rd Div.	As above.	"Y" Bde H.Q. to STEENWERCK
Aug. 16th.	M.G.Coys & Lt T.M.Batteries 23rd Div.	Transport Lines	Trenches.	M.G.Coys & Lt T.M.Batteries 41st Div.	Transport Lines	M.G.Coys & Lt T.M.Batteries will proceed under Bde arrangements to Billets in Reserve Area.
	Adv. Parties, "X" & "Y" Bdes 23rd Div.	-	Trenches.	-	-	
	2 Bns, "Y" Bde 23rd Div.	STEENWERCK Area.	LE BIZET and ARMENTIERES.	2 Bns, 123rd Inf. Bde.	LA CRECHE Area.	
	122nd Inf. Bde	LA CRECHE Area.	METEREN Area.	-	-	Bde H.Q. to METEREN.
	9th S.Staffs Regt. (P).	COURTE CROIX.	STEENWERCK Area.	-	-	

DATE.	UNIT.	FROM.	TO.	IN RELIEF OF.	TO.	REMARKS.
Aug. 17th	122nd Inf.Bde	METEREN Area	FLETRE Area.	-	-	
	2 Bns, 123rd Inf. Bde.	LA CRECHE Area	MONT DES CATS Area	-	-	Relief to commence at 5 a.m. Bde H.Q. do not move.
	"X" Bde, 23rd Div.	PAPOT, SOYER, CRESLOW.	Trenches.	124th Inf. Bde	PAPOT, SOYER, CRESLOW.	Relief to commence at 9 p.m. H.Q. 123rd Inf. Bde to RABOT.
	2 Bns, "Y" Bde 23rd Div.	LE BIZET and ARMENTIERES.	Trenches.	2 Bns, 123rd Inf. Bde.	Bivouac near NIEPPE - PONT D'ACHELLES Rd.	
	2 Bns, "Y" Bde 23rd Div.	STEENWERCK Area.	LE BIZET and ARMENTIERES	2 Bns, "Y" Bde, 23rd Div.	Trenches, as above.	
	"Z" Bde, 23rd Div.	Reserve Area.	STEENWERCK Area.	-	-	"Z" Bde H.Q. to STEENWERCK.
	9th S.Staffs Regt (P).	STEENWERCK Area.	OOSTHOVE FARM.	19th Middx R. (P).	Square A 3.	To billet or bivouac under arrangements to be made by 124th Inf. Bde.
Aug. 18th.	"Z" Bde, 23rd Div.	STEENWERCK Area.	PAPOT, SOYER, CRESLOW.	124th Inf. Bde.	METEREN - STEENWERCK Area.	To be completed by 12 noon. 123rd Inf. Bde H.Q. to MONT DES CATS Area. "Z" Bde H.Q. to B 10 a 5 5. 124th Inf. Bde H.Q. to STEENWERCK.
	2 Bns, 123rd Inf. Bde.	Bivouac on NIEPPE - PONT D'ACHELLES Rd.	MONT DES CATS Area	-	-	To be clear of PONT D'ACHELLES by 12 noon.

DATE.	UNIT.	FROM.	TO.	IN RELIEF OF.	TO BILLET AT.	REMARKS.
	B. ROYAL ENGINEERS.					
	3 F'd Coys 23rd Div. To be arranged by C.R.E.'s 23rd & 41st Divs.	Reserve Area.	41st Div. Area.	228 F'd Co. R.E. 233 " " " 237 " " "	FLETRE Area. MONT DES CATS Area. STEENWERCK Area.	To be arranged by 122 I.B. " " " 123 " " " " 124 "
	C.— R.A.M.C.					
	3 F'd Ambs. 1 San. Sec. To be arranged by A.D.M.S. 23rd and A.D.M.S. 41st Div.	Reserve Area.	41st Div. Area.	138 F'd Amb. 139 " " 140 " " 84th San.Sec.)	FLETRE Area. MONT DES CATS Area. STEENWERCK - METEREN Area.	To be arranged by 122 I.B. " " " 123 " " " " 124 "
	D.— A.S.C.					
	4 Coys, 23rd Divl Train. Under Orders of A.A.& Q.M. G's 23rd & 41st Div.	Reserve Area.	41st Div. Area.	41st Divl Train. H.Q.Company. No. 2 " No. 3 " No. 4 "	H.ETRE. FLETRE Area. MONT DES CATS Area. METEREN Area.	Under orders 122 I.B.Group. " " 123 " " " " 124 " "
	E. DIVL HEADQUARTERS.					
Aug. 17th.	D.H.Q. & 23rd Divl Signal Coy	FLETRE.	STEENWERCK.	D.H.Q.& 41st Divl Signal Coy.	FLETRE.	

DATE.	UNIT.	FROM.	TO.	IN RELIEF OF	TO BILLET AT.	REMARKS.
F. A.V.D.						
As arranged between A.D.V.S. 23rd & 41st Divs.	Mob. Vet. Sec. 23rd Div.	Reserve Area.	PONT D'ACHELLES.	52nd Mob. Vet. Sec.	STEENWERCK - METEREN Area.	Under arrangements to be made by 124th Inf. Bde Group.

The LA CRECHE Area is contained in Squares A 3, 4, 5, and 6 (less billets and horse standings occupied by Divl Train, R.A. and Infantry Transport) and is available for units of the 41st Div. for bivouac or halting places, under arrangements to be made by A & Q, 41st Div.

SECRET.   Copy No. 15.

EXPLANATORY NOTE to 41st DIVISION ORDER No. 35.

                                                    13-8-16.

1.-   With reference to 41st Division Order No. 35 of
        to-day, Brigades of 23rd Division have been detailed as
        follows:-

                "X" Brigade.   - 70th Infantry Brigade.
                "Y"   "   - 68th   "   "
                "Z"   "   - 69th   "   "

2.-   Machine Gun Companies and Trench Mortar Batteries will
        be relieved as follows:-

        70th M.G. Coy & Light T.M. Battery will relieve 124th M.G.
                                      Coy & Light T.M. Battery.
         68th   do.   do.   will relieve 123rd Do. do.
         69th   do.   do.   will relieve 122nd do. do.

3.-   Please acknowledge.

                                                H.M. Wilson
                                                   Major, G.S.

                Copy No. 1 - Fifth Corps.
                  "   " 2 - 36th Division.
                  "   " 3 - New Zealand Division.
                  "   " 4 - Fifth Corps H.A.
                  "   " 5 - 23rd Div. "G".
                  "   " 6 - 23rd Div. "Q".
                  "   " 7 - "Q".
                  "   " 8 - C.R.A.
                  "   " 9 - C.R.E.
                  "   " 10 - 122nd Inf. Bde.
                  "   " 11 - 123rd   "   "
                  "   " 12 - 124th   "   "
                  "   " 13 - 19th Middx R. (Pioneers).
                  "   " 14 - A.D.M.S.
                  "   " 15 - 41st Divl Signal Coy.
                  "   " 16 - 171st Tunnelling Coy, R.E.
                  "   " 17 - 1st Australian Tunnelling Coy.
                  "   " 18 - "M" Coy, 3rd Bn, Special Bde R.E.
                  "   " 19 - File.
                  "   " 20 - War Diary.
                  "   " 21 - Spare.
                  "   " 22 - Spare.
                  "   " 23 - Spare.

                                ack d

SECRET.   Copy No. 12.

41st DIVISION ORDER No. 38.

20-8-16.

1.-   The 41st Division will proceed by rail on August 23rd and 24th to join the Fourth Army.

2.-   All orders and instructions for entrainment etc. will be issued by A & Q, 41st Division.

3.-   On arrival in the Fourth Army Area the 41st Division will be attached to the Tenth Corps (temporarily).

4.-   The 41st Division Report Centre will close at FLETRE at 2 p.m. on 24th instant and open at AILLY LE HAUT CLOCHER at the same hour.

5.-   Acknowledge.

H M Wilson
Major, G.S.

Issued at 6 a.m. as under:-

         Copy No. 1 - IX Corps.
           "   "   2 - X Corps.
           "   "   3 - "Q".
           "   "   4 - "Q".
           "   "   5 - C.R.A.
           "   "   6 - C.R.E.
           "   "   7 - 122nd Inf. Bde.
           "   "   8 - 123rd   "   "
           "   "   9 - 124th   "   "
           "   " 10 - 19th Middx R. (P).
           "   " 11 - A.D.M.S.
           "   " 12 - 41st Divl Signal Coy.
           "   " 13 - File.
           "   " 14 - War Diary.
           "   " 15, 16, 17 - Spare.

Vol 5

41 Div. Signal
Coy. R.E.

War Diary

September 1916.

Army Form C. 2118

4/Div. Signal Coy. R.E.

WAR DIARY or INTELLIGENCE SUMMARY

(Erase heading not required.)

Instructions regarding War Diaries and Intelligence Summaries are contained in F.S. Regs., Part II. and the Staff Manual respectively. Title Pages will be prepared in manuscript.

Place	Date	Hour	Summary of Events and Information	Remarks and references to Appendices
AILLY LE HAUT CLOCHER	1/9/16		Divisional Artillery left PONT REMY for 15th Corps area. Capt. Elsdale, 3 operators, 3 linemen and 2 DRs leave with them.	
	5/9/16		Office relief with Lighting set, office stores etc. leave in lorry for BUIRE. Lorry returns when unloaded.	
			All horses, wagons etc. proceed under Lt. Patrick at 10.30 am. for ARGUEVES.	
	6/9/18		2/Lt Jefferies followed at 8 pm. The whole transport of the division march today for 15 Corps area. Dismounted units travel by tactical trains in 6th & 7th insts.	
BUIRE SUR L'ANCRE			The Company continued march and arrived at BUIRE SUR L'ANCRE at 6.30 pm. Divisional report centre opened BUIRE SUR L'ANCRE at noon – through to XV Corps at HEILLY on Sounder & 'phone, no other lines, except locals to G.O. etc. 16 men proceeded by train, remainder of office by train, lorry left AILLY at 2 pm with office relief & stores. Lorry left behind to keep Signal office open. 1 NCO, 1 O.T., 1 Clerk & 1 DR.	
"	7. Sept		Old office at AILLY closed at 10 am.	
	9 Sept.		1 2 3 Rels moved to bivouac near FRICOURT. 1 2 4 Rels " " " " " BECORDEL. Owing to inability to complete that state of readjustment many dispatches are being carried by mounted orderlies.	

WAR DIARY or INTELLIGENCE SUMMARY

Army Form C. 2118

Place	Date	Hour	Summary of Events and Information	Remarks and references to Appendices
BUIRE SUR L'ANCRE	10/9/16		Div. Office relief sent to BELLEVUE FARM the ready. Stall war 11/9/16 from 55th Division.	
BELLEVUE FARM	11/9/16		Office opened at 9 am. 123 I. Bde is in the line with their HQ at POMMIERS REDOUBT. 122nd & 124th Bdes are in support & reserve. There are no wires to them.	
	14/9/16		122nd & 124th Bde move up to YORK TRENCH & take over the line held by 123 Bde. See diary attached of operations 14th — 17th. Traffic totals of telegrams 15th inst. 883 telegrams / 16th inst. 776 " / 17th inst. 860 "	
	18/9/16		Division relieved by 55th Div. & moved back to RIBEMONT. 21st D.A. remain in the line. 2 Lt. C.J. Jefferies & one cable section remain for Artillery purposes.	
RIBEMONT	25/9/16		From 12.35 pm division is under two hours notice to move.	
	28/9/16			
	30/9/16		123 H Bde are attached to 21st Division. Situation remains the same.	

W.O. Burnet Rhynehart Capt. for Lt. Col. Signal Eng. R.E.

1875 Wt. W593/326 1,000,000 4/15 J.B.C. &A. A.D.S.S./Forms/C. 2118.

Army Form C. 2118

WAR DIARY
or
INTELLIGENCE SUMMARY
(Erase heading not required.)

Place	Date	Hour	Summary of Events and Information	Remarks and references to Appendices
Field	22/8/16		The following casualties occurred during the month of Sept. '16.	
	5/9/16		1 O.R. evacuated to Casualty Clearing Sta.	
	9/9/16		No 524 Pte Davies R.H. transferred from 20th (S) Bn. D.L.I. to R.E. as a Pioneer	
			2 N.C.Os (Pioneer) reported as Sappers (Telegraphists Field Line).	
	13/9/16		1 O.R. joined as reinforcement from Base Signal Depot.	
	14/9/16		2/Lt. W.G. Spencer joined from 15th Corps Sig. as Supernumerary.	
	15/9/16		1 O.R. wounded & evacuated.	
	"		Lieut. John MACKRETH killed in action.	
	22/9/16		2 O.R. wounded by shell fire & evacuated.	
			2/Lt. R.L.G. Goldsmith R.E. joined from XV Corps Sig. vice Lieut. J. Mackreth.	
	25/9/16		3 O.R. joined as reinforcements from Base Signal Depot	

W. Murphy Munhead
Capt.
O.C. 41 Div Signal Coy R.E.
1/10/16.

SECRET.   COPY NO. 12th

                    41st Division Order No. 37.
                                            5
                                          4/9/16.

1.   The 41st Division (less Artillery, 2 Field Coys R.E. and
        Pioneers) will move to the XV Corps Area about DERNANCOURT.

2.   Dismounted personnel (including Lewis Gun Detachments and
        T.M.Batteries) by train on 6th and 7th instant under instructions
        to be issued later.

3.   The 1st Line and Train Transport, bicycles and led horses of
        all units and formations, with the exception of 124th Infantry
        Brigade Group, under the Command of Lt-Col. Molony, A.S.C., will
        proceed by Road on 5th inst, to billet night 5th/6th at ARGOEUVES
        and LONGPRE in accordance with attached March Table.

4.   124th Inf. Bde. Group Transport will move to BOUCHON and
        MOUFLERS on night 5th/6th as per March Table. Instructions for
        move on 6th inst. will be forwarded later.

5.   The Transport Columns, with the exception of 124th Inf Bde
        Group, will continue their march on 6th inst. to DERNANCOURT
        under orders to be issued by O.C. Column : Route AMIENS - QUERRIEU
        - D 12 d 8.8. - DERNANCOURT. Head to reach QUERRIEU at 11 a.m.
        where they will halt and water.
              An Officer and cyclists will be sent on in advance to report
        to Camp Commandant 4th Army QUERRIEU to arrange halting and
        watering places.

6.   During the March ¼ mile intervals will be maintained between
        units and ½ mile intervals between Groups.

7.   A Senior Major will be detailed to Command each Brigade Group
        - Lt-Col Molony will command Divl. H.Q. Group in addition to
        Column.

8.   Horsed Field Ambulances will march in rear of each of their
        Groups.
              In addition 3 Motor Ambulances will leave AILLY LE HAUT
        CLOCHER at 3 p.m. and will follow the Route of Transport Column
        to deal with men who have fallen out.

9.   Billeting Parties of 1 Officer per Group and 1 N.C.O. and 2
        cyclists per unit will report to A.A. & Q.M.G. 41st Div. at
        Church ARGOEUVES at 3 p.m.

10.   Completion of move and position of H.Q. of O.C. Column and
        Brigade Groups will be reported to Div. H.Q.

11.   Acknowledge.

                                              H.M.Wilson
                                                Major G.S.

Issued at 1 a.m.

                                          ack'd

Issued to :-

Copy No. 1 - X Corps.
" 2 - XV Corps.
" 3 and 4 Q 41st Div.
" 5 - C.R.A.
" 6 - C.R.E.
" 7 - 122nd Inf.Bde.
" 8 - 123rd Inf.Bde.
" 9 - 124th Inf.Bde.
" 10 - 19th Middx R. (P).
" 11 - A.D.M.S.
" 12 - 41st Div. Sig. Co.
" 13 - 237th Fd. Co. R.E.
" 14 - Lieut-Col. Molony A.S.C.
" 15 - Camp Commandant.
" 16 - File.
" 17 - War Diary.
" 18 - Spare.

MARCH TABLE to accompany 41st. Divisional Order No. 37

UNITS	Starting Point	Time to be clear by.	Route	To Halt for water at	To bil-lot at	REMARKS
Transport of 122 I.B. Group 122 Bde. H.Q. 4 Battns 122 M.G.Coy. No.2 Co.Div.Train 138th Fd.Amb.	LA FOLIE, on AILLY-FLIXECOURT Road 2 miles N.W. of FLIXECOURT	11 a.m.	FLIXECOURT - BELLOY - ST. SAUVEUR	BELLOY	LONGPRE	Coys. of Divisional Train, Mob. Vety. Section, and H.Q. & 1 Section 237th Fd. Coy. R.E. will join their respective Columns at FLIXECOURT.
Transport of 123rd I.B.Group 123rd Bde.H.Q. 4 Battns 123rd M.G.Co. No.3 Co.Div.Train 139th Fd.Amb.		11.45 a.m.		BELLOY	LONGPRE	
Div.H.Q.Group Div.H.Q. 41st Div.Sig.Coy. H.Q. & No.1 Div.Tn. Mob.Vet.Section 237th Fd.Coy.R.E. less 1 Sect.		12.30 p.m.		FLIXECOURT	ARGOEUVES	
124th Inf.Bde.Group 124th Bde.H.Q. & 4 Battns. 124th M.G.Co. No.4 Coy.Div.Train 140th Fd.Amb.		Billets by 2.30 p.m.	AILLY LE HAUT CLOCHER		MOUFLERS & BOUCHON	Billets to be arranged by 122nd Inf. Bde. No.4 Coy.Train will not move

Francport-ST

SECRET.   Copy No. 12

41st DIVISION ORDER No. 38.

5-9-16.

1.- The dismounted personnel of 122nd and 123rd Inf. Bde Groups, Divisional Headquarters and 237th Field Company, R.E., (less 1 Section) will proceed by tactical trains to XVth Corps Area on 6th instant.
   The dismounted personnel of 124th Inf. Bde Group will follow by tactical trains on 7th instant.
   Entraining Station - LONGPRE-LES-CORPS-SAINTS.
   Detraining Station - MERICOURT.

2.- All orders and time tables for entrainment will be issued by 'A & Q, 41st Division.

3.- On arrival, units and formations will proceed to Camps, as under:-
   Divisional H.Q.)
   Sanitary Section) ....Camp in D 28 d (¾ mile West of BUIRE SUR ANCRE).
   122nd Inf. Bde Group.....Camp in E 9 a & c.
   123rd   "   "   "   ..... " near BECORDEL.
   124th   "   "   "   ..... " in E 9 a & c.
   Divl Train and)
   Mob. Vety Section) ..... " on BUIRE - DERNANCOURT Road,
   where their transport will join them under arrangements to be made by O.C. Column.

4.- SUPPLIES.
   Refilling for 122nd and 123rd Inf. Bde Groups and for Divl H.Q. Group for rations for consumption on the 7th inst. will take place at square E 7 c on evening of 6th or early morning of 7th.
   For 124th Inf. Bde Group (rations for consumption on the 8th) refilling will be at the same place on evening of 7th or early morning of 8th.

5.- Completion of move and positions of H.Q. of units and formations (giving co-ordinates) will be reported to Divl H.Q.

6.- An Advanced 41st Div. Report Centre will open at Camp D 28 d at noon, 6-9-16. The Report Centre at AILLY LE HAUT CLOCHER will close at 10 a.m. on 7-9-16.

7. Acknowledge.

                                                   Major, G.S.

Issued at 5 p.m., as under:-
Copy No. 1 - Xth Corps.   Copy No. 11 - A.D.M.S.
   "   " 2 - XVth Corps.   "   " 12 - 41st Divl Signal Coy.
   "   " 3 & 4 - "Q", 41st Div.   "   " 13 - 237th Field Co. R.E.
   "   " 5 - C.R.A.   "   " 14 - Lt.-Col. MOLONY, A.S.C
   "   " 6 - C.R.E.   "   " 15 - Camp Commandant.
   "   " 7 - 122nd Inf. Bde.   "   " 16 - File.
   "   " 8 - 123rd   "   "   "   " 17 - War Diary.
   "   " 9 - 124th   "   "   "   " 18 - 19 and 20 - Spare.
   "   " 10 - 19th Middx R. (P).

SECRET.   Copy No. 18

41st DIVISION ORDER No. 39.

Ref. Map: GUILLEMONT, 1/20,000.   10-9-16.

1.-   The 41st Division will take over the Centre Sector of the XVth Corps front from COCOA LANE (exclusive) to the junction of TEA TRENCH and PEACH TRENCH (inclusive).

2.-   The 123rd Infantry Brigade will relieve portions of the 165th and 166th Infantry Brigades on the above front and will be distributed as follows:-
         FRONT LINE - 2 Battalions.
         SUPPORT... - 1 Battalion.
         RESERVE... - 1 Battalion.
Relief to be complete by 8 a.m., 11th September. All arrangements for relief will be made between Brigades concerned.

3.-   The 122nd Infantry Brigade will move into Camp at FRICOURT (F 14 a), as Brigade in support, as soon as that Camp is vacated by 123rd Infantry Brigade - Route: via the horse track N. of the DERNANCOURT - MEAULTE - FRICOURT Road. Distances of 500 yards to be maintained between Battalions.
         123rd Infantry Brigade will inform 122nd Infantry Bde when Camp will be clear.

4.-   The 124th Infantry Brigade will remain in its present Camp at BECORDEL, and will become Brigade in Divisional Reserve.

5.-   All moves E. of FRICOURT will be by Companies at 300 yards distance, and troops will keep to tracks as far as possible, so as to clear the roads.

6.-   The boundaries of the Sector will be as follows:-

(a) NORTHERN. (between 41st Division and New Zealand Division) Junction of TEA TRENCH and PEACH TRENCH (S 11 b 60.35) (inclusive to 41st Div.) - Junction of PEAR STREET and PLUM STREET (S 11 c 85.55) - WEST YORK ALLEY - Junction of WEST YORK ALLEY and CARLTON TRENCH (S 16 b 25.35) (all exclusive to 41st Div.) - S 16 d 0.6. - S 22 a 0.0.

(b) SOUTHERN. (between 41st Div. and 164th Inf. Bde, 55th Div.) Junction of front line and COCOA LANE (S 12 d 65.85) - COCOA LANE and LONGUEVAL ALLEY (exclusive to 41st Division) - S 18 b 20.85 - S 23 a 71.76. - CRUCIFIX ALLEY (exclusive to 41st Div.) - Railway at S 22 d 3.5.

S.18.c 28.85

(c) Boundary between XVth and XIVth Corps will be - Junction of GUINCHY AVENUE with FRONT LINE, about T 13 c 75.15. - thence to S 24 b 85.85. - thence to S 24 b 0.8. - trench junction S 24 a 0.6. (inclusive to XVth Corps) - road junction S 23 d 9.1. (exclusive to XVth Corps)

7.-   The G.O.C., 41st Division, will assume command of the Centre Sector and the remainder of the XVth Corps front between COCOA LANE (inclusive) and GUINCHY AVENUE (inclusive), including the 164th Inf. Bde, 55th Division, holding that front, at 9 a.m. on September 11th.

/2.-

8.- The completion of all moves and reliefs will be reported to Divisional Headquarters by telegram.

9.- The 41st Division Report Centre will close at BUIRE (D 28 d) at 9 a.m., 11th September, and open at the same hour at BELLEVUE FARM (E 5 c).

10.- Acknowledge.

B.L. Anley
Lt.-Colonel, G.S.

Issued at **2** p.m., as under:-

Copy No. 1 - XVth Corps.
" " 2 - 55th Div.
" " 3 - Guards Div.
" " 4 - New Zealand Div.
" " 5 - XVth Corps H.A.
" " 6 - 21st H.A.G.
" " 7 - 33rd H.A.G.
Copies Nos. 8 & 9 - "Q", 41st Div.
Copy No. 10 - 122nd Inf. Bde.
" " 11 - 123rd " "
" " 12 - 124th " "
" " 13 - 134th " "
" " 14 - C.R.A.
" " 15 - C.R.E.
" " 16 - 19th Middx R. (Pioneers).
" " 17 - A.D.M.S.
" " 18 - 41st Divl. Signal Coy.
" " 19 - File.
" " 20 - War Diary.
Copies Nos. 21, 22 & 23. - Spare.

SECRET.   41st Div.
                    G. 117
                    67/13.

122nd Inf.Bde.	41st Div.Signal Co.
123rd Inf.Bde.	A.D.M.S.
124th Inf.Bde.	A.D.V.S.
C.R.A.	D.A.D.O.S.
C.R.E.	A.P.M.
"Q"	

Ack

    It is notified for information that the NEW ZEALAND DIVISION will take over the left sector, XV Corps Front on night 10/11 September.   FRONTAGE from Junction TEA TRENCH and PEACH TRENCH to Junction WOOD LANE and CORK TRENCH.
    Divisional Headquarters E 11 Central.

10/9/16

                                     Major, G.S.

SECRET.   Copy No. 15

41st DIVISION ORDER No. 40.

Ref. Map: GUILLEMONT, 1/20,000.   11-9-16.

1.- The 14th Division will relieve the 41st Division right, from T 13 central to COCOA LANE (inclusive) on Sept. 12th/13th.

2.- The 41st Inf. Bde will relieve the 164th Inf. Bde on the above front. All arrangements for relief will be made between those Brigades.
The 41st Inf. Bde will come under the command of the G.O.C. 41st Division on entering the Divisional area, and will then report its position by telegram to H.Q. 41st Division.

3.- Boundaries will be as follows:-
Between 41st Inf. Bde and Guards Division.
T 13 central - PILSEN LANE (inclusive to 41st Inf. Bde) - S.E. corner of DELVILLE WOOD (inclusive to 41st Inf. Bde) - Northern corner of TROMES WOOD (inclusive to Guards Div.) - S 22 d 9 1.
NOTE: The Guards Division has handed over STOUT Trench and GINCHY AVENUE temporarily, for the use of a Battalion in support of the PILSEN LANE garrison, if required.

Between 41st Inf. Bde and 123rd Inf. Bde, 41st Division.
COCOA LANE (inclusive to 41st Inf. Bde) - S 18 a 0.0. - S 25 a 6.7. - S 22 c 8 2.

4.- The G.O.C. 41st Division will hand over command of the line from T 13 central to COCOA LANE (inclusive) to G.O.C. 14th Division at 8 a.m., 13th instant.

5.- The completion of all moves and relief, and the transfer of command will be reported to H.Q. 41st Division.

6.- Acknowledge.

B L Anley
Lt.-Colonel, G.S.

Issued at 8 p.m., as under:-
```
Copy No. 1 - XVth Corps.
  "   "  2 - 55th Div.
  "   "  3 - Guards Div.
  "   "  4 - 14th Div.
  "   "  5 - XVth Corps H.A.
  "   "  6 - 21st H.A.G.
  "   "  7 - 23rd H.A.G.
Copies  "  8 & 9 - "Q", 41st Div.
Copy No.10 - 123rd Inf. Bde.
  "   " 11 - 124th
  "   " 12 - C.R.A.
  "   " 13 - C.R.E.
  "   " 14 - A.D.M.S.
  "   " 15 - 41st Divl Signal Coy.
  "   " 16 - File.
  "   " 17 - War Diary.
  "   " 18 - New Zealand Div.
Copies Nos.
     19 & 20 - Spare.
```

Ack'd

SECRET.   Copy No... 12

41st DIVISION ORDER No. 44.

Map Ref: 57c S.W., 1/20,000.   14-9-16.

1.- The following road is allotted to the 41st Division for repairs, in the advance:-
   Horse track from MONTAUBAN about S 27 a 2 0 to where it joins the track leading from S 28 a 5 2, through S 22 d,b, and S 17 a,c to LONGUEVAL.
This is to be made capable of taking all horsed transport.

2.- The 19th Middlesex (Pioneers) are detailed to carry out the above work, which will be commenced punctually at zero hour on the 15th Sept. All holes will be filled in as quickly as possible.

3.- When roads and tracks have been made complete to LONGUEVAL, work will be concentrated on the LONGUEVAL - FLERS road, and when this is completed, a forward and return track for wheeled transport must be made ready to GUEUDECOURT.

4.- As soon as these roads are repaired for horse traffic, the following will be taken in hand by the C.E., XVth Corps, with a view to making them suitable for Mechanical Transport:-
   (a) Road BERNAFAY WOOD to LONGUEVAL.
   (b) "   LONGUEVAL to FLERS.
   (c) "   LONGUEVAL to BAZENTIN.

6.- Acknowledge.

5.- Wagons and G.S. limbered wagons for tools to accompany Battalion to area of assembly near MONTAUBAN.

                                                           B L Anley
                                                         Lt.-Colonel, G.S.

Issued at   a.m., as under:-

   Copy No. 1 - XVth Corps.
    "   " 2 - 14th Div.
    "   " 3 - New Zealand Div.
    "   " 4 - C.R.A.
    "   " 5 - 122nd Inf. Bde.
    "   " 6 - 123rd   "   "
    "   " 7 - 124th   "   "
    "   " 8 - 19th Middx R. (P)
    "   " 9 - C.R.E.
    "   " 10 - "Q".
    "   " 11 - A.P.M.
    "   " 12 - 41st Divl Signal Coy.
    "   " 13 - War Diary.
    "   " 14 - File.
    "   " 15 - O.C., Divl Yeomanry Troop.
    "   " 16 - A.D.M.S.
   Copies 17 to 20 - Spare.

SECRET.   Copy No...... 14

41st DIVISION ORDER No. 41.

15-9-16.

1.- The 123rd Inf. Bde will be relieved on Sept. 13th/14th by 122nd and 124th Inf. Bdes: relief to be complete by 6 a.m., 14th inst.

2.- 124th Inf. Bde will take over the Right Sub-Sector from COCOA LANE (exclusive) to FLERS Road (exclusive), with 1 Battalion in front line, 1 Battalion in support, half 124th Machine Gun Company and half 124th Trench Mortar Battery.

3.- 122nd Inf. Bde will take over the Left Sub-Sector from FLERS Road (inclusive) to junction of PEACH TRENCH and TEA TRENCH (inclusive), with 1 Battalion in front line, 1 Battalion in Reserve, and half 122nd Machine Gun Company and half 122nd Trench Mortar Battery.

4.- 2 Battalions, half 122nd M. G. Coy and half 122nd T. M. Battery, 122nd Inf. Bde, will remain in FRICOURT CAMP.
2 Battalions 124th Inf. Bde, half 124th M. G. Coy and half 124th T. M. Battery, will move from BECORDEL to FRICOURT CAMP, as soon as vacated by 2 Battalions, 122nd Inf. Bde.

5.- On relief, 123rd Inf. Bde will be distributed in MONTAUBAN ALLEY, CATERPILLAR TRENCH, BEETLE TRENCH, FRITZ TRENCH and POMMIER TRENCH.

6.- Headquarters of Brigades after relief will be as follows:-
122nd Inf. Bde)
124th "   ") in YORK TRENCH.
123rd "   "   POMMIERS REDOUBT.

7.- The boundary between 122nd and 124th Inf. Bdes will be S 22 c 8 6 to cross roads S 17 b 3 4 (inclusive of FLARE LANE) - thence via LONGUEVAL - FLERS Road to road junction at S 6 b 9 3.

8.- All moves East of FRICOURT will be by companies at 300 yards distance.

9.- The completion of reliefs will be reported to Divl Headquarters by telegram.

10.- Acknowledge.

B L Anley.
Lt.-Colonel, G.S.

Issued at 12.30 a.m. to,

achd

P.T.O.

SECRET.   Copy No........

                    Copy No. 1. - XV Corps.
                       "   " 2. - 14th Division.
                       "   " 3. - New Zealand Divn.
                       "   " 4. - XV Corps H.A.
                       "   " 5. - 21st H.A. Group.
                       "   " 6. - 23rd H.A. Group.
                       "   " 7. - "Q", 41st Divn.
                       "   " 8. - "Q", 14th Divn.
                       "   " 9. - 122nd Inf Bde.
                       "   " 10. - 123rd Inf Bde.
                       "   " 11. - 124th Inf Bde.
                       "   " 12. - C. R. A.
                       "   " 13. - A.D.M.S.
                       "   " 14. - 41st Div Signal Coy.
                       "   " 15. - File.
                       "   " 16. - War Diary.
                       "   " 17. - C. R. E.
                       "   " 18. -)
                       "   " 19. -) Spare.
                       "   " 20. -)

SECRET. Copy No...9...

41st DIVISION ORDER NO. 43.

Ref. Map 57c S.W.
1/20,000.
14/9/16.

1.   In addition to the operations mentioned in 41st Division Order No. 42 dated 13/9/16, it is notified that the 14th Division will on the 15th September, clear of all enemy the area BEER TRENCH - BITTER TRENCH - East edge of DELVILLE WOOD - HAYMARKET - HOP ALLEY - ALE ALLEY as far east as T 13 a 8 9 and the new trench running from T 13 a 8 9 to about T 13 b 0 5.

2.   Every effort will be made to complete the operation before Zero in order that the attack on the main objectives may go forward unhindered.

3.   The area to be cleared, will be bombarded tomorrow [today] by heavy howitzers, provided air observation is possible.

4.   Acknowledge.

Lt.Colonel. G.S.

Issued at 1.55 a.m.

Copy No. 1.   -   XV Corps.
"   "   2.   -   New Zealand Div.
"   "   3.   -   C. R. A.
"   "   4.   -   122nd Infantry Bde.
"   "   5.   -   123rd   "   "
"   "   6.   -   124th   "   "
"   "   7.   -   C. R. E.
"   "   8.   -   19th Middlesex Regt.
"   "   9.   -   41st Div. Signal Coy.
"   "   10. -   " Q ".
"   "   11. -   War Diary.
"   "   12. -   File.
"   "   13, 14, 15 - Spare.

DIARY OF COMMUNICATIONS,
15th. SEPTR., 1916.

WIRELESS.

Nothing to report.   No messages received.

PIGEON SERVICE.

6.53 am.   Message from BEAR addressed to POPPY.   Timed 6.10 am.

8.2 am.   Message from SCUD addressed to SCAN. Timed 7.30 am.

8.29 am.   Message from SKIN addressed to SCAN. Timed 7.55 am.

9.0 am.   Message from SKIN addressed to SCAN. Timed 8.40 am.

9.48 am.   Message from SCOT addressed to SCAN. Timed 9.28 am.

10.30 am. Message from SCUD addressed to SCUD. Timed 10.2 am.

10.38 am. Message from SKEW addressed to SCAN. Timed 10.35 am.

11.2 am.   Message from HOGG addressed JEWEL. Timed 10.25 am.

11.10 am. Message from 2nd. German Line (sender not stated) addressed to JAY.   Timed 10.30 am.

11.20 am. Message from JACKDAW addressed to JAY. Timed 10.45 am.

11.44 am. Message from Capt. S.E.J.Elliott, R.H.A. addressed to STAFF CAPTAIN.   Message untimed.

12.8 pm.   Message from LOVE addressed to LOCK. Timed 11.50 am.

12.46 pm. Message from D Company, LORD, addressed to 3rd. Brigade.   Timed 12.10 pm.

1.35 pm.   Message from SKIN addressed to SCAN. Timed 12.45 pm.

4.28 pm.   Message from Lieut. ARNOLD addressed to H.Q., 41st. Division.   Timed 3.35 pm.

MAJOR, R.E.,
A.D.A.S., XV Corps.

16th. Septr., 1916.

Issued to :
    O.C., Signals, 14th. Division.
                   41st. Division.
                   55th. Division.
                   N.Z. Division.
    XV Corps Wireless Officer.
    XV Corps Pigeon Svce. Officer.

Copies, for information, to :
    XV Corps "O".
    D.D.A.S., 4th. Army.

"A" Form. Army Form C. 2121.
MESSAGES AND SIGNALS.

Prefix ......Code......m	Words	Charge	This message is on a/c of:	Rec'd. at ......m
Office of Origin and Service Instructions.	Sent		Service.	Date
	At......m			From 7.IX.16
	To		(Signature of "Franking Officer.")	By
	By			

TO ~~C.R.A. C.R.E. QUAIL. JAY. POPPY. BLOCK.~~
~~19th Middx. A.D.M.S. 41st Div Sigs. D.A.D.O.S.~~
~~A.P.M. Camp Cmdt. 21 Div. N.Z. Div. 55 Div. 15~~
A A A Corps.

Sender's Number.	Day of Month.	In reply to Number.	
G.701	17th		

Ref 41st Div Order No 45 of 17/9/16 paras. 8 and
15 for 7 a.m. read 9 a.m.

From 41st Div.
Place
Time 8-30 p.m.

The above may be forwarded as now corrected. (Z)
(sd) H.H. Wilson
Censor. Signature of Addressee or person authorised to telegraph in his name.
* This line should be erased if not required. Major G.S.

SECRET.   Copy No. 12

41st DIVISION ORDER No. 45.

REF: 1/10,000 Map, "British Front   17-9-16.
from HIGH WOOD to GINCHY."
1/40,000 ALBERT sheet.

1.-   The 41st Division and 64th Inf. Bde (less Artillery) will be relieved by the 55th Division on the 17th/18th Sept., in accordance with attached Table of Reliefs.

2.-   Preliminary instructions have been sent by wire to those immediately concerned.

3.-   The 41st Divl Artillery Group, now covering the front of the 41st Division, will come under the orders of the 55th Division from the hour of taking over command.

4.-   Troop, R. Wilts Yeo., come under the orders of the G.O.C., 55th Division at the same hour.

5.-   On arrival in the 41st Division area on the 17th/18th Sept., all units of the 55th Division will come under the orders of the G.O.C. 41st Division until the command passes.

6.-   (a)   All details of relief, as to time etc., to be arranged between the Brigades etc. concerned.
      (b)   C.R.E. to arrange with C.R.E. 55th Division for relief of Field Companies and Pioneer Battalion.
      (c)   A.D.M.S. to arrange with A.D.M.S. 55th Division for relief of Field Ambulances.
      (d)   Relief of all other Administrative units to be arranged by "Q" Branch, 41st Division.

7.-   Units, after relief, will be assembled between MONTAUBAN and MAMETZ, and will move by the fair weather track N. of the RIBEMONT - FRICOURT Road in small bodies.

8.-   (a)   Trench map, air photo, and Brigade Dumps of S.A.A., grenades etc., to be handed over, under arrangements to be made between the Infantry Brigades concerned.
      (b)   "Q" Branch to arrange for handing over of Divl Dump of S.A.A., grenades etc.
      (c)   Lists of code addresses and code books for use with Wireless etc., and copies of instructions for their use, will not be handed over but will be kept for future use.

9.-   The command of the front held by the 41st Division will pass to the G.O.C. 55th Division at 7 a.m., 18th inst.

10.-   Completion of relief by each formation, unit, etc., to be reported by telegraph to Divl H.Q., at which hour relieving Commander will assume command.

11.-   All Light Trench Mortar Battery personnel and all Stokes Guns will accompany the 41st Division on relief.

12.-   On completion of relief -
      (a)   The 41st Division will assemble:-
            122nd Inf. Bde Group - AREA E.
            123rd   "   "   " - BECORDEL.
            124th   "   "   " - AREA E.
            Divl H.Q............ - RIBEMONT.
            R.E. & 19th Middx R. - FRICOURT CAMP.

/(b)

(b)   64th Inf. Bde, at present attached to 41st Division, will rejoin its own Division.

13.-   41st Division Report Centre will close at BELLEVUE FME at 9 a.m., 18th inst. and reopen at same hour at RIBEMONT.

14.-   Acknowledge

B.L. Anley
Lt.-Colonel, G.S.

Issued at 1.30 p.m., as under:-

  Copy No. 1 - File.
  "   "   2 - War Diary.
  Copies 3 & 4 - "Q".
  Copy No. 5 - C.R.A.
  "   "   6 - C.R.E.
  "   "   7 - 122nd Inf. Bde.
  "   "   8 - 123rd   "   "
  "   "   9 - 124th   "   "
  "   " 10 - 19th Middx R.
  "   " 11 - A.D.M.S.
  "   " 12 - 41st Divl Signal Coy.
  "   " 13 - D.A.D.O.S.
  "   " 14 - A.P.M.
  "   " 15 - Camp Commandant.
  "   " 16 - 21st Division.
  "   " 17 - New Zealand Div.
  "   " 18 - 55th Division.
  "   " 19 - XVth Corps.
  "   " 20 - O.C., Troop R. Wilts Yeo.
  Copies 21 to 26 - Spare.

Date.	Relieving Unit.	Unit to be relieved.	From	To	Remarks.
17/18 Sept.	165th Inf.Bde.	64th Inf.Bde.	Front Line.	CAMP near POMMIER Redoubt.	
	166th Inf.Bde.	123rd Inf.Bde. Group less R.E.Coy.	FLERS. FLERS Trench.	BECORDEL	166th Inf.Bde to take over defences of FLERS Village.
		124th Inf.Bde. Group less R.E.Coy.	SWITCH Trench & original line.	Area E.	
Morn 18th.	164th Inf.Bde.	122nd Inf.Bde. Group less R.E.Coy.	SAVOY, CARLTON YORK Trenches.	Area E.	Relief to commence at 5 a.m. 18/9/16.
17/18 Sept.	3 Field Coys 55th Div.	3 Field Coys. 41st Div.	MONTAUBAN.	FRICOURT CAMP.	
17/18 Sept.		19th Middlesex R.	MONTAUBAN.		

DIARY OF COMMUNICATIONS, 16-9-16.

WIRELESS.

    1.10 am. Corps Station reports "In constant communication with Sets Pkk, PG and PI".

PIGEON SERVICE.

    11.29 am. Message from JAY addressed to JEwEL. Timed 11.10am.

    12.43 pm. Message from SKIN addressed to SCAN. Timed 12.10 pm.

    1.20 pm. Message from Observation Officer, FLERS VILLAGE, addressed to 41st. Division. Timed 12.35 pm.

                                          MAJOR, R.E.,
17-9-16.   A.D.A.S, XV Corps.

            Issued to :

            O.C., Signals,
                14th. Division.
                41st. Division.
                55th. Division.
                21st. Division.
                N.Z.Division.
            XV Corps wireless Officer.
            xV Corps Pigeon Svce. Officer.

            Copies, for information, to :

            xV Corps "G".
            D.D.A.S, 4th. Army.

War Diary

REPORT ON SIGNAL COMMUNICATIONS during OFFENSIVE
OPERATIONS 14th - 17th Septr 1916.

Units & locations.
The 41st Div. formed part of the 15th Corps, which was at Heilly. The 41st Div. H.Q. was established at BELLEVUE FARM, rather more than 8 miles behind our front line and about 7miles behind the Brigades in action.
The 122nd and 124th Infy. Bdes. were the Bdes. in action the front lines, with their H.Qs. in a dugout in York Trench about 2000 yds behind our front line; the 123rd Bde were in reserve with their H.Q. established at in Pommiers Redoubt.

In addition, the 21st Div. Arty was cooperating in the attack and was under the orders of the C.R.A. 41st. Div. - and on the evening of the 15th, the 64th Infy. Bde. was also attached to the Division.

General System of Lines.

Lines were promised by A.D.A.S. 15th Corps as follows;
4 prs between Bellevue Farm and Pommiers.
5 prs between Pommiers and York Trench, this was the minimum I considered necessary to carry the heavy traffic expected, which it must be remembered included the Arty of two Divisions, and later an additional Infy Bde.

All Arty lines radiated from Pommiers Redoubt, and as this was the place to which the Division would move in case of an advance, and was also a Bde. H. Q. An advanced Signal Office and Exchange was established there under Lieut. Patrick.

All circuits personnel and instruments were arranged on the assumption that the above lines allotted to the Div. by the Corps would be available and in working order.-

It was obvious on the 13th Septr. that the Corps lines from Pommiers to York Trench would not be ready till well on in the day of the 14th Septr, and as the 122nd and 124th Bdes. were to move up there some time on the 14th there was nothing left but to lay our own lines

This was done by a detachment working under Capt. Elsdale who left camp at 4-0 a.m.

Two prs were laid in the Corps trench and were through by 6-0 p.m. which was the time ordered by the General Staff.

That day Lieut. Patrick was busy establishing the Office at Pommiers. Important telephone circuits such as Ammunition Dump, Grenade Dump, were put through, and in addition numerous other circuits C.R.E. A.D.M.S. Div. Train. etc.

I was advised on the 14th that the new Corps buried lines would be handed over to us at 4-0 p.m. actually they were handed over to Lieut. Patrick about 4-0 a.m. 15 Septr. and then only two single lines were found to be good and workable, out of five pairs promised.

Between Pommiers and Bellevue Farm on the morning 15th Septr, out of four pair promised two pairs were good, one pair was faulty and could only be used for telegraph, the remaining pair was not handed over till the afternoon of the 16th.

On the 16th inst two more pairs between Pommiers and York Trench were put through still leaving us deficient of two pairs promised.

On the 17th inst a good pair was substituted for the faulty pair between Pommiers and Bellevue, and another pair up to York Trench was put through.

Thus by the evening 17th inst we were still deficient of one of the pairs promised between Pommiers and York Trench.

Traffic.

The traffic was very heavy. 883 Telegrams alone being dealt with on the 15th inst, many of these were verylong - the longest being Operation Orders consisting of over 360 words while a large number were over 150.

The privilege of writing "priority" telegrams was apparently very much abused, nearly all Arty. wires were marked "priority" and in one case the telegram was a weekly return, reporting deficiencies on horse transport, another a daily ammunition return.

Many messages were unnecessarily long and were not written in telegraphic language but rather after the fashion of a written report.

Arty. Formations were again the chief offenders and this tended to block up the wires unnecessarily

A case occured on the 15th of a letter addressed to the 41st Div. and marked urgent being handed in to the Pommiers Signal Office. This was opened and found to contain an officers application for leave.

Wireless;

Was not used.

Visual.

Was not used between Bdes. and Div.

Pigeons.

Were used successfully and brought some valuable information. One case occurred of Pigeons being "tossed" before the attck commenced and when there was telephonic communication close by.

Another time it would probably be better if all available birds were sent up to battalions.; reinforcements of pigeons sent up to battalions after an advance of a mile had been made got lost and at least one case occurred of pigeons being flown close up to the front line, without any messages, and at a time when information of the situation was badly wanted.

D. Rs.

Despatch Riders were able to ride their machines right up to Bde. H.Qs. as the weather was fine. Had the weather been wet this would not have been possible and arrangements were made to have some mounted orderlies and runner posts to relay important messages on.

Eight mounted orderlies were posted at Pommiers Redoubt and full use was made of these, mostly in local delivery work.

COMMUNICATION IN FRONT OF BRIGADES.

Each Bde. had wires close up to the assembly trenches and only one or two faults occurred on their lines. Intermediate Offices at about 300^X interval were established along the route, and linemen were posted at these points. Two Runners or Guides were also posted there.

At the end of the wires, 6 runners were posted. These posts were pointed out to all Btn. Signal Officers and Signallers.

After the advance had started messages were brought back to these posts and were telephoned on to Bde. H.Q.

On the 16th inst wire was run out and reached into Flers village; but this did not hold up owing to shell fire. Runner posts were established by the left Brigade, but how far these were used is not clear. In the case of the left Bde 3 Btn. Signal Officers became casualties early in the operations.

VISUAL. Visual with venetian blind shutters were tried in one case, but was evidently seen by the enemy, as the result was that the place where they were was almost immediately shelled.

A visual station was established by the right Bde in front of Delville Wood and was close by the telephone wire to Brigade H.Qs. but this station did not pick up any battalion stations.

ATTACHED BRIGADE.

The 64th Bde. 21st Div. was attached to the Div. from the evening of 15th inst; their H.Q. was first established at Pommiers - later moving up to York Trench. About noon on the 16th I learnt that the Bde had moved their H.Q. up into Switch Line; I at once sent some men up to York Trench to a cable and establish communications with them, but on arriving up there myself I found that the Brigade were doing it themselves and were just completing the line. The Signal Officer of this Bde. did not come and report to me as he should have done, nor did I receive any communication from him whatsoever, respecting the movements of his brigade.

1. For good and rapid communication the Div. must be closer up. Good talking on the telephone over the distance on the lines and material that one has in the field is more than can be expected.

SIGNALLING TO AEROPLANES. Messages must be curtailed as much as
po

Some messages were sent by battalions, but as received by the aeroplane were for the most part unintelligible. The aeroplane dropped the bag at BRUCAM PO but was only picked up by a Frenchman two days later.

One interesting case is recorded. The 11th. Btn. Queens captured a prisoner who stated that the enemy were going to counter attack at 2-0'clock.

When the contact aeroplane came over, the Btn, signalled in the panel and asked if enemy were concentrating to attack. Aeroplane asked in what direction On being answered "Flers" aeroplane sent back "No everything normal.".

Conclusion.

In conclusion I would like to make the following remarks.

1. For good and rapid communication the Div. must be closer up. Good talking on the telephone over the distance on the lines and material that one has in the field is more than can be expected.

2. Messages must be curtailed as much as possible and restrictions put on senders of priority telegrams.

3. Sufficient accomodation must be provided beforehand for Signal Offices. The Offices in York Trench and Pommiers Redoubt were every overcrowded and tended to delay the enormous pressure of work experienced.

4. All units must report their whereabouts to the nearest Signal Office, to facilitate the delivery of messages and save much time being wasted looking for individuals and units.

5. Bdes. should settle beforehand the position of their next H.Qs. so that preparation may be made before they move.

6. Runners; It would seem that runners could be divided into two headings (1) Guides, (2) relay post for communication in case of wires lines or other means failing.

To be successful these posts must be very carefully organised, more especially in an advance, and I think to be successful requires the undivided attention of an officer. A Bde. Sig. Officer has many things to do, (a) organising and supervising his own office, (b) planning out new lines to be laid (c) organising pigeons personnel, (d) visual stations, (e) sometimes a wireless station. I recommend that an officer should be told off to organise and look after the runner posts either working under the Bde. Signal Officer or in the closest possible touch with him.

M. Raye Trunkard Capt
OC 41 Div Signal Coy

DIARY OF COMMUNICATIONS,
17 - 9 - 1916.

WIRELESS.

    1.32 pm. Corps Station reports "Communication established with N Z Station PCC at 11.29 am. and with 14th. Divnl. Station PH at 11.15 am. Good signals now with all five stations".

    6.11 pm. Corps Wireless reports "Position of PCC S 6 b 5.3."

PIGEON SERVICE.

    10.29 am. Message from SPUR addressed to SPAR. Untimed.

    11.15 am. Message from 12 N F addressed to 62nd. Infantry Brigade. Timed 10.40 am.

    1.55 pm. Message from AUGER addressed to ACID. Message timed 11.0 am.

    2.30 pm. Message from QUIET addressed to JEWEL. Timed 2.16 pm.

    3.20 pm. Message from PEAR addressed to POPPY. Timed 2.45 pm.

    3.55 pm. Message from PEAR addressed to POPPY and PEAR. Timed 3.20 pm.

    5.0 pm. Message from Sigs., BLOCK addressed to CHISEL. Timed 4.10 pm.

    5.12 pm. Message from BLOCK addressed to TOOLS. Timed 4.31 pm.

18-9-16.

MAJOR, R.E.,
A.D.A.S., XV Corps.

Issued to :
  O.C., Signals, 14th. Division.
               21st. Division.
               41st. Division. ✓
               55th. Division.
               N. Z. Division.
  XV Corps Pigeon Service Officer.
  XV Corps Wireless Officer.
Copies, for information, to:
  XV Corps "G".
  D.D.A.S., 4th. Army.

Vol 6

WAR DIARY

41 Div. Sig. Coy. R.E.

October 1916.

Army Form C. 2118

41 Div Signal Coys

WAR DIARY or INTELLIGENCE SUMMARY

(Erase heading not required.)

Place	Date	Hour	Summary of Events and Information	Remarks and references to Appendices
RIBEMONT	1/10/16		2/Lt. Spencer with 1 NCO & 10 men left for CARLTON TRENCH to lay new line in Corps trench to the Adv. Bde HQ. Where 122 Bde will be established.	
RIBEMONT	3/10/16		Lt Patrick left for Carlton Trench Signal Office to establish Office. Capt Elsdale left for Fricourt Chateau to prepare Office for Div HQ. All the Company (less 2 NCO's, 2 cooks & DR's) left for Fricourt Camp	
FRICOURT CHATEAU	4/10/16	9 am	Office opened at 9 am. 15 Corps have allotted up 4 pairs from Fricourt to Pommier Redoubt and 3 pairs from there up to York Trench. Units as follows - 122 Bde holding the front line - 124 Bde in support at Carlton Trench - 123 Bde near Mametz Wood in reserve. Communication as follows 'phone to 123 Bde - Sounder & 'phone to 124 Bde, direct 'phone and Buzzer between Carlton Tr. Office & Bde. Owing to bad state of roads motor cyclists cannot go in front of Div HQ. All work has to be done by DR's Mounted on horses.	
	5/10/16		Lt ~~Ted~~ Pain on the field cable pair from Pommier to CARLTON Tr. and Ted with it at 233rd Fd Cy near Mametz is enabling CAFE to get all Fd Corps via Carlton Tr. Orderlies from there also deliver to premier Bn and "S" Lines premiere who are attached to us. Owing to the wet a drift the corps having formed of Carlton Tr has fallen in and our 2 GP lines have been broken and have taken the whole day to relay or repair. This has held up work from S6A8? forward to new Blighty living hutt at S36c 3½ ½	

WAR DIARY
or
INTELLIGENCE SUMMARY
(Erase heading not required.)

Army Form C. 2118

Place	Date	Hour	Summary of Events and Information	Remarks and references to Appendices
FRICOURT CHATEAU	5/10/16	contd	with the result that only 1 pair has been laid and that has stopped STD× short of the new Hq.	
	6/10/16		Laid two pairs down went portion of corps loop, one from S6a77 Hq, and the other direct from S6a1d line in continuation of one of our existing prs. Both we intended to reach new Bde Hq, building in N36c 3½. 2. but failed by about STD×. The pair between the latter and the new Hq was completed very heavy shelling all day at N36c 3½. ½ caused interruption of work; and the portion completed was frequently broken. Working parties from here to 122 Bde at French trench on enough current at with 50 cell each end. This owing to inability to keep portion of line long enough to get a DR through to Cullaty. First all telly wks; any length of tether; any way which has been done on a line on a later length. But it latter line ¾ communication to new Hq at N36c 122 Bde	
	7/10/16		As we call not guarantee safe communication to new Hq. Zero hour 1-45 pm. stayed in French trench. While 114 Bde Hq do went. Working duplex to corps. At 12-30 pm our buried line about 3 to 6 pm. Working duplex by wonder and Wypher. 123 Bde moved to Cullen trench ‐ communication by runners and letters we failed and that we no no mins delay in any message. Sent ordinary Wypher calls Falk had to wait a considerable time.	

Army Form C. 2118

WAR DIARY
or
INTELLIGENCE SUMMARY
(Erase heading not required.)

Instructions regarding War Diaries and Intelligence Summaries are contained in F.S. Regs., Part II. and the Staff Manual respectively. Title Pages will be prepared in manuscript.

Place	Date	Hour	Summary of Events and Information	Remarks and references to Appendices
FRICOURT CHATEAU	9/10/16	6.p.m	123 Bde take over left Sub-Sector from 122 Bde. Their H.Q. change places i.e. 123 Bde move to FERRET TRENCH and 122 Bde to CARLTON TRENCH. 123 Bde will move tomorrow to their new H.Q. at M30a 3½.½. Where 2/Lt Spencer has today succeeded in laying by different routes 2 pairs BD5 cable — speaking through from Divl H.Q. is found — distance is 6½ m. Great difficulty has been experienced in getting the heavy D5 cable drums up — they have to be carried nearly two miles up to the Bde H.Q. Some form of light skeleton wooden drum should be improvised —	
"	9/10/16	4·20pm	A quiet day as regards traffic in the wires. 2 lines in front of Front Tr Hq to 123 Bde Hq have been down — repaired — and have given no signs again owing to shelling. The men have been working 4am to 6pm and 6am to 8pm the last two days under difficult conditions and are tired. Today Wilson is out attempting to lay field lines Forward to QUAIL (123).	
BUIRE	11/10/16	10 pm	A quiet day yesterday. Laid a ladder line from Front Tr to M30c 2½·½. Considerable movement in this evening due to the relief and consequent X messages Trouble all day owing to the people using sections of our lines when cutting our own out in some cases. Our relief by the	

1875 Wt. W593/826 1,000,000 4/15 J.B.C. &A. A.D.S.S./Forms/C. 2118.

WAR DIARY or INTELLIGENCE SUMMARY

Army Form C. 2118

Place	Date	Hour	Summary of Events and Information	Remarks and references to Appendices
BUIRE	14/10/16	10 pm	The 30th Div was completed today. Command passed at 10 am. 41 Div now disposed as follows. HQ BUIRE with Tel to Corps. 122 Bde Sig Sta a message by DR from FRICOURT (30th Div). 123 Bde (Telephone to 30 div). 122 HQ 421 FBC (Telephone to 30 div) 124 HQ 421 FBC No incident at present. Communication normal. Communication this morning before leaving the area.	
"	15/10/16		122 Bde moved to E14 central (approx) to establish new Signal Office by DR.	
HALLEN- COURT	16/10/16		Lorry left for HALLENCOURT with one relief. Advn. Div. Report opened at HALLENCOURT at noon. The Company left BUIRE at 8.15 am and marched to ARGOEUVES.	
	17/10/16		Company arrived HALLENCOURT at 6 pm.	
	18/10/16		Divn HQ at HALLENCOURT. The division is now located as follows: 122 Bde at LIMERCOURT. 123 Bde " HOCQUINCOURT. 124 Bde " ARRAINES. Telephone lines to all Bdes thro' the ARRAINES Exchange existing through the Civil Exchange	

Army Form C. 2118

WAR DIARY
or
INTELLIGENCE SUMMARY
(Erase heading not required.)

Instructions regarding War Diaries and Intelligence Summaries are contained in F.S. Regs., Part II. and the Staff Manual respectively. Title Pages will be prepared in manuscript.

Place	Date	Hour	Summary of Events and Information	Remarks and references to Appendices
HALLEN COURT	19/10/16		The Company marched at 6.30 am to entrain at PONT REMY for 2nd Army area - lorry left same time with MT's, and 3 men for FLETRE but established Div. Sig. Office there.	
FLETRE	20/10/16		The Company detrained at GODEWAERSVELDE about 1-0 am and marched to FLETRE. Signal Office opened 10 am, through to 1st ANZACS on telegraph and 9th Corps in 'phone. 123 Pole arrive Godewaersvelde and 124 Pole at METEREN. 'phone communication to each - 122 Pole - arrive and billet at EECKE. (phone).	
"	21/10/16		124 Pole move to Boeschepe.	
"	22/10/16		1 Officer, 2 Signal masters and 6 linesmen left for RENINGHELST to learn lines, office etc of 4th Aust. Div - from whom we take over in 24 hrs.	
"	23/10/16		123 Pole go into front line & come under 4th Aus'ln Div. 124 Pole moved into front line on 22.9 night.	
RENINGHELST	24/10/16	NOON	Division Signal Office opened noon, when the command passed from 4th Aust. Div - to 41st Division. 123 Pole are in the left - 124 Pole in the right. Pole HQ at BURGOMASTERS FARM and LA CLYTTE. Aust. Div "C" & "E" in reserve at ONTARIO CAMP. The 13th Aust. Pole superimposed signaller and telephone circuits to all Brigades -	

Army Form C. 2118

WAR DIARY
or
INTELLIGENCE SUMMARY
(Erase heading not required.)

Instructions regarding War Diaries and Intelligence Summaries are contained in F.S. Regs., Part II. and the Staff Manual respectively. Title Pages will be prepared in manuscript.

Place	Date	Hour	Summary of Events and Information	Remarks and references to Appendices
REMNG HEUST	25/10/16		13 Aust. Bde in reserve are relieved by 122 Inf Bde.	
"	29/10/16		122 Inf Bde relieve 123 Inf Bde in the left sector. The Pdr. Sections do not relieve each other, it being considered that the Communications with result of Pdr Sections relieve independently of the Brigades and not oftener than once a fortnight.	
"	31/10/16		The situation remains unaltered.	

W Murgatroyd Capt
O.C. 41 Div. Signal Coy R.E.

31/10/16.

Army Form C. 2118

WAR DIARY
or
INTELLIGENCE SUMMARY
(Erase heading not required.)

Instructions regarding War Diaries and Intelligence Summaries are contained in F.S. Regs., Part II. and the Staff Manual respectively. Title Pages will be prepared in manuscript.

Place	Date	Hour	Summary of Events and Information	Remarks and references to Appendices
Field	1/10/16		3 O.R. arrived from Base Signal Depôt as reinforcements.	
"	7/10/16		1 O.R. wounded in action & evacuated.	
"	10/10/16		2 O.R. evacuated sick.	
"	11/10/16		4 O.R. arrived from Base Signal Depôt as reinforcements.	
"	20/10/16		Lieut. Wm. Patrick granted leave to United Kingdom to 29/10/16.	
"	24/10/16		2 O.R. arrived from Base Signal Depôt as reinforcements.	
"	24/10/16		2 O.R. evacuated sick.	

W Murray Trumbull
Captain
O.C. 4th Signal Coy/R

1/11/16.

REPORT ON 41st. DIV. SIGNAL COMMUNICATIONS during

OFFENSIVE OPERATIONS OCTOBER 5th - 11th.

At 9 a.m. on the 5th. 41st.Div, Office opened at FRICOURT CHATEAU. At that hour the lines allotted to the Div. by 15th Corps Signals were put through both forward to POMMIERS REDOUBT and back to E11 CENTRAL, and 15th CORPS. IN front of POMMIERS the existing N. Z. Div. communications were taken over.

Owing to the complicated nature of the change it was impossible to have our lines working before the N. Z.Div office shut down. For this reason it was two or three hours before our communications settled down to a satisfactory state of efficiency Everything was quite ready and had been tested correct from FRICOURT before hand as far as POMMIERS.

Two of the causes in delay in getting properly going are perhaps worth quoting. One was that though speech to CARLTON TRENCH Sig. Office was good, it was bad to the 124th Bde Staff less than 100 yards away. This being entirely unexpected a little time elapsed before a new line was fixed up; the men being busy settling down.

The other case was delay in getting good speech with the 122nd Bde.at FERRET TRENCH. This was owing to the necessity of testing out each section of all the different routes available before the best through line could be got. The speaking when obtained was I think, good, and was certainly better than the previous division had ever obtained.

One telephone call from FERRET TRENCH was put through to 15th Corps at HEILLY (H.Q.) and the speaking was quite clear.

At no time during operations was there any delay on "Priority" telegrams, or even ordinary telegrams on the main routes, i. e. Div. H.Q. to Bde. H. Q.

Taking into consideration the heavy shelling forward and the absence of any existing system of communication beyond FERRET TRENCH it was considered advisable to send two officers and every available man to form a strong working party at CARLTON TRENCH.

This formed the advanced Div. Sig. Office, and from there traffic could be regulated and sent by whichever lines were working at any given time.

As it was the party there had an exceedingly strenuous time and had to ease off a little on the 9th as so many were going sick utterly exhausted. Owing to this concentration of men at CARLTON TRENCH we were very shorthanded elsewhere.

For this reason the change in position of the 123rd Bde. H. Q. from CARLTON TRENCH to MAMETZ WOOD after all our working parties had gone out involved considerable delay in telephonic communication being established.

There were no existing lines that culd be made use of.

New lines were laid to the Div. Dump near POMMIERS and to the 233rd Field Co. R. E. who took messages for all the R. E. Field Coys, and Pioneers.

For two days before we took over we had been laying and improving lines to FERRET TRENCH in anticipation of other Bdes. moving up and to better the existing lines. The result being that though we had on an average one disconnection per hour day and night we never lost touch with this station.

Communication with the Bde. H.Q. at M.30.c.3½.½. took a long time to establish satisfactorily.

This was due to the following facts:-

(1) "That the shelling round this H. Q. was continually breaking lines as they were laid.
(2) "That it took 3½ hours to carry up the heavy cable drums from CARLTON TRENCH during the bad weather and that the hardest work on the men came in the transport of the stores, not in laying and maintaining lines.
(3) "That the Corps Cable trench constructed by our Pioneer Btn. was unfortunately sited as it ran between battery positions. It was also too wide and was used as a communication trench and was continually shelled. It also fell in, in many places owing to the wet.

After the 123rd Bde. moved up to this advanced H. Q. communication by buzzer was once lost for two hours, but the telephone was out of use about 30% of the time. However the urgent calls for "G" branch were successfully put through on the buzzer line, though the speaking naturally suffered.

BRIGADES.
The area in front of Bde. H. Q. was constantly subjected to heavy shell fire. But prior to the 7th the Bde. in the line managed to keep lines through to Btn. H. Q. for most of the time.

On the 7th however it was found impossible to do more than maintain one system forward to a central advanced Bde. Sig. station whence runners took messages to the different Btn. H. Q. near by.

D.R.L.S.
For the geater part of the time Motor Cycles were useless in from of FRICOURT. D.R.L.S. therefore went by mounted orderly to CARLTON TRENCH and thence by runner. Considerable delay on messages was therefore unavoidable.

VISUAL.
Communication from Flers to CARLTON TRENCH was successfully maintained but the telegraph never failed and only test messages were sent.

Visual was used in some cases between Bde. H. Q. and Btn. H. Q. but more often from Btn. H. Q. forward.

PIGEONS.	Pigeons were successfully used. Some birds took very considerably longer time than others probably owing to their not having been properly watered.
SIGNALLING TO AEROPLANES.	Touch was obtained with the contact aeroplane by some units, but it appears no messages were actually sent on the signalling panel.
ARTILLERY.	The Artillery covering our front were the 21st Div. Artillery and the N. Z. Div. Artillery and were the same as before and after the 41st. Div. came out of the line. Their system of communications was therefore unchanged and was run by personnel found by their own Divisions.

[signature] Capt.
O.C. 41 Div. Sig. Coy R.E.

SECRET. 41st Div.
G.769
(34/9)

ORDERS REGARDING SIGNAL COMMUNICATIONS
FROM 4th OCTOBER, 1916.

TELEGRAPHS & TELEPHONES.   1.- An Advanced Divisional Signal Office with telephone exchange will be established at CARLTON Trench. This office will be telegraphic and telephonic communication with Divnl H.Q. and all Infantry Brigades.

WIRELESS.   2.- Wireless offices will be established at the Advanced Brigade Office, S 6 a 8.7., and the CARLTON Trench office, both in touch with the Corps wireless station at POMMIERS.

VISUAL.   3.- A chain of visual stations will be established between FLERS and CARLTON Trench at the following points :- M 36 b 6.2., S 6 c 6.6., S 5 d 3.2., S 16 b 3.3. Messages for transmission to the Division can be handed in at any of these points.

D.R's.   4.- Dispatch riders to the advanced brigade will proceed by day to FLERS Dump, where the brigade will establish a Runner Post to take despatches in to the Brigade. By night or in bad weather, D.R's will go to CARLTON Trench office, where despatches will be handed over to the Runner Post furnished by the 123rd Infantry Bde.
   If the roads become impassable for motor cyclists, mounted D.R's may have to be used from FRICOURT.

MARKING RUNNER POSTS.   5.- A quantity of yellow canvas has been issued to Brigade Signal Officers. This is intended to be cut up and stuck on posts to mark the positions of Runner Posts and if necessary, forward Brigade H.Q's.
   Some form of lamp (for Brigade, red lamp) should be placed outside these posts at dusk to assist runners and D.R's to find the way. These could be shielded from the enemy.

PIGEONS.   6.- Pigeons will be brought by Divnl Signals to CARLTON Trench and Brigades will be responsible for conveying birds forward to battalions. The number of birds per Brigade will vary with the number of Brigades in the line, but when the three Brigades are in the line, each Brigade will probably get 8 birds. There will be 4 for the Divnl Observation Officer.

CIRCUIT DIAGRAM.   7.- Circuit diagrams have been issued to all Signal Officers.

3rd October, 1916.

                               Lt.-Colonel, G.S.

Issued to all recipients of 41st Division Warning Orders Nos. 4 and 5.

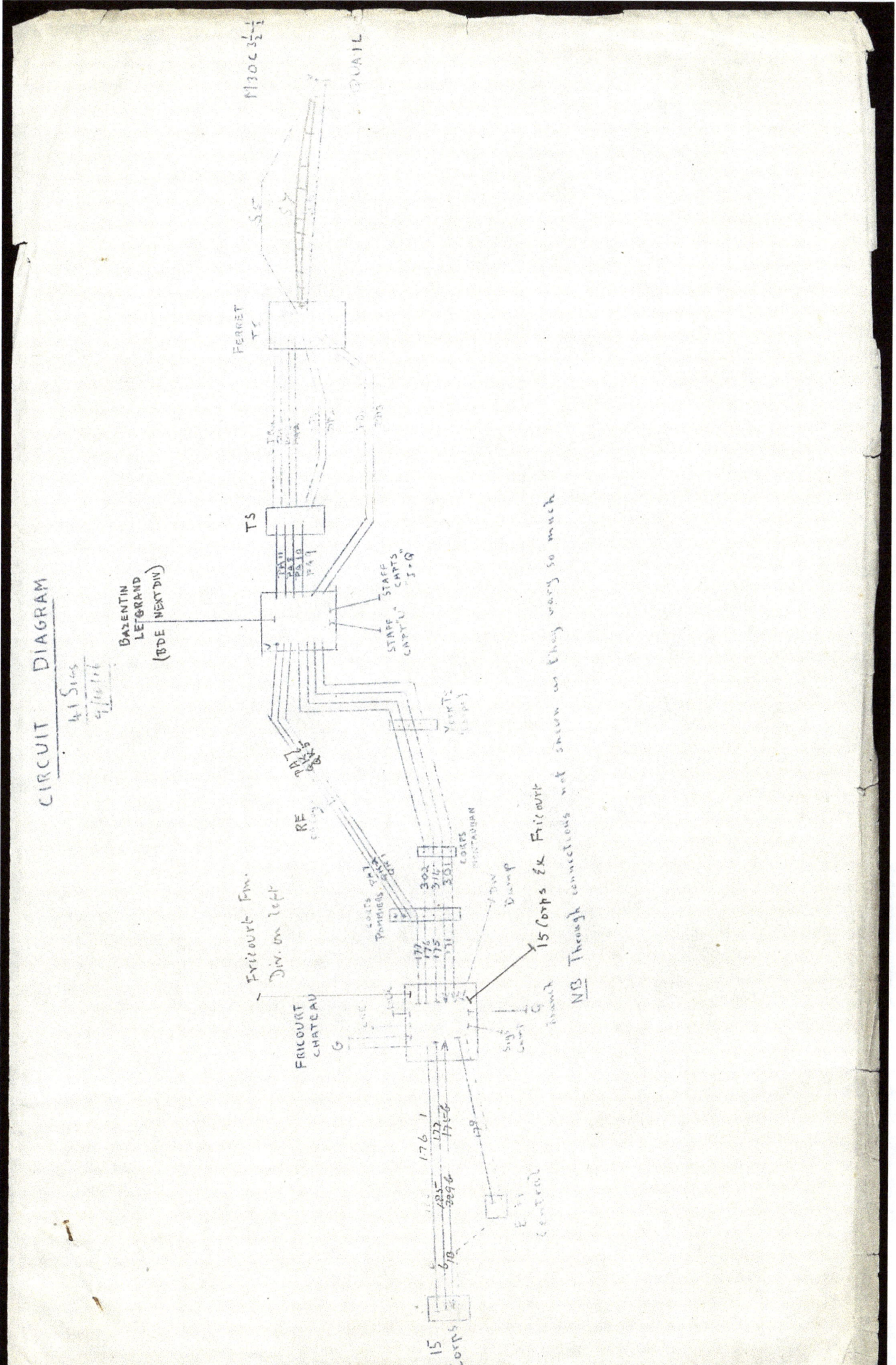

COMMUNICATIONS
21st D.A.

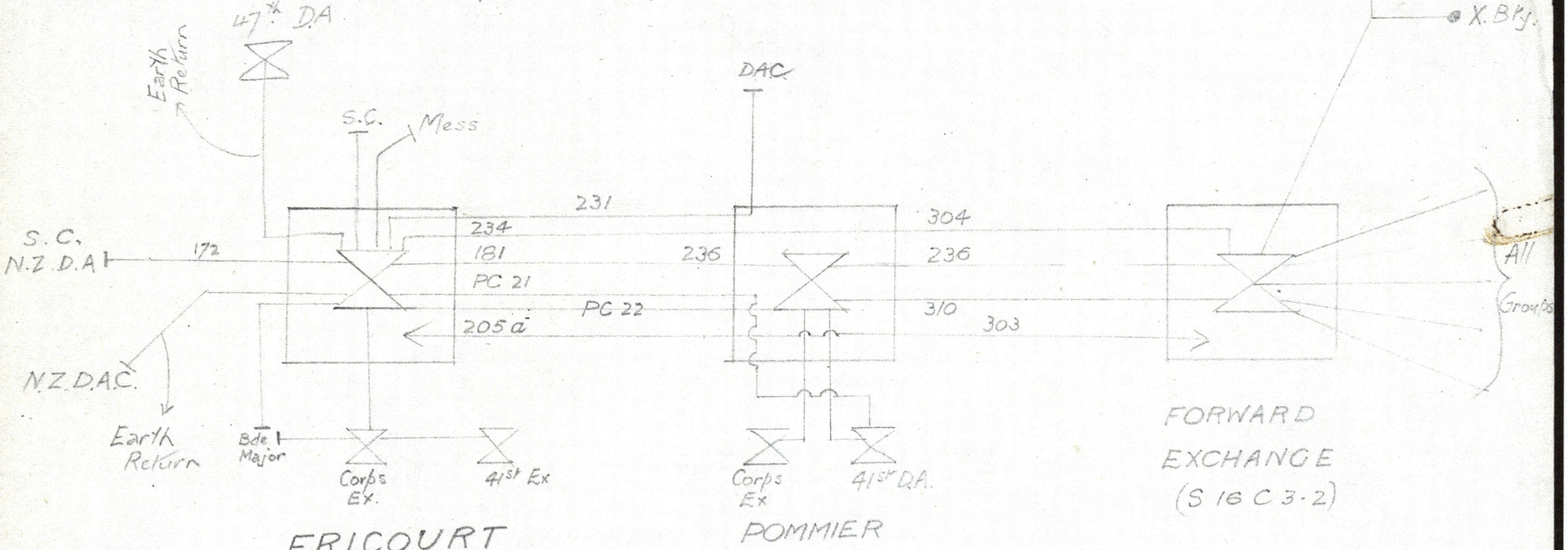

(Hand-drawn schematic diagram of communications network)

Labels on diagram:

- N. Bty
- X. Bty
- 47th D.A
- A/1
- Groups
- FORWARD EXCHANGE (S 16 C 3·2)
- DAC
- 304, 236, 310, 303
- 41st DA
- Corps Ex
- POMMIER
- 231, 236
- PC 21, PC 22
- 234, 181, 205a
- S.C. Mess
- Bde Major
- 41st Ex
- Corps Ex.
- FRICOURT
- S.C. N.Z.D.A1
- N.Z.D.A.C.
- Earth Return
- 172

Group HQ

94 Bde Gp	S 12 & 5·2
95 "	S 17 6 7·4
1st NZ "	S 6 a 4·7
2nd " "	S 6 + 6·5
3rd " "	S 18 c 4·3
4th " "	S 18 c 4·3

DIARY OF COMMUNICATIONS.

PERIOD- 30-9-16 to 7-10-16.

WIRELESS.

7-10-16. Communication as follows:

        41st Div.   P C C   S6 b45
                     P K K   S16 c98

        12th Div.   P H   S6 d81
                     P G)
                     P I) At disposition of
                                  Divisional Signal Officer.

PIGEON SERVICE.

Messages received as follows:

Date	Time Despatched	Time Received	From	Addressed to
5th Oct.	8- 30 am	9- 10 am	JAY	JEWEL
6th Oct.	4- 3 pm	4- 40 pm	KALE	KATE
	4- 55 pm	6- 0 pm	KALE	KATE
7th Oct.	4- 6 pm	4- 55 pm	Harry Barnard B H Q	JAY
	Untimed	5- 0 pm	JAM	JAY
	3- 25 pm	5- 5 pm	Harry Barnard B H Q	JAY
	3- 5 pm	3- 55 pm	JAM	JAY
	10- 20 am	11- 24 am	PEPPER	POPPY
	2- 40 pm	3- 1 pm	KEEP	KATE
	2- 40 pm	3- 18 pm	G S O 3rd D A B	D A B
	Untimed	4- 0 pm	JACKDAW	JAY
	2- 30 pm	4- 10 pm	KEEN	KATE
	4- 35 pm	5- 9 pm	D A B Staff Officer	D A B
	4- 0 pm	4- 55 pm	Divisional O B Officer	JEWEL

O 1½ hrs (longest time)
X 34 mins (shortest time)

                                          MAJOR R. E.
8-10-16   A.D.A.S. XV CORPS

        Issued to   Signals ~~12th Div.~~
                               41st Div.
                               ~~30th Div.~~
        ~~XV Corps Pigeon Service Officer~~
        ~~XV Corps Wireless Officer~~

        ~~For information to ...~~ XV Corps "G"
                               ~~D.D.A.S. 4th Army.~~

O longest time
X shortest time

"A"

General Basis. 1. Reference 41st Div. G.224 (34/29) dated 21/10/16, in order to give effect to the principles of training therein described, the following will be the basis on which training is to be carried out :-

Infantry Battalions will continue to train men as Signallers up to a certain standard, when they have reached this standard they will be sent to the Brigade Signalling School, where they will receive further training; when passed as efficient by the Brigade Signal Officer they will be sent back to their Units.

Initial Training by Units. 2. The training which signallers are to receive in their own Units is as follows :-
  (1) Morse Alphabet.
  (2) Reading and sending on flags, lamp, shutter disc, and buzzer up to 4 words per minute.

Units to continue training as many men as possible as above, and will endeavour to reach a higher standard if possible.

Brigade Schools. 3. When men have reached the standard as described in para 2. they will be sent to the Brigade School. The numbers to be maintained at the School should be about 24, i.e. 6 from each Battalion. The course at the Brigade School will normally be about 1 Month, but a certain amount of latitude will probably have to be allowed.

The training to be carried out at Brigade Schools will be as follows :-

Working hours - 8 hours per day with one half day per week.

  (1) Reading and sending on flag, lamp, shutter disc, up to 8 words per minute, reading and sending on buzzer up to 12 words per minute.
  (2) Station discipline - transmitting stations.
  (3) Simple cable laying.
  (4) Reconnaissance of routes for cables.
  (5) Cable in trenches; buried cable - poled cable.
  (6) Different types of cable.
  (7) Maintenance of lines - labelling of lines.
  (8) Test boxes - junction boxes.
  (9) Testing lines - leaky lines.
  (10) Fault finding.
  (11) How to arrange and set up an office.
  (12) Office procedure.
  (13) Lectures on elementary electricity and magnetism.
  (14) Instruments - D.3's, Fullerphones, Jambing buzzers, listening sets, French Daylight Lamps, buzzer exchanges.
  (15) Care and use of instruments - how to test instruments.
  (16) Induction - overhearing.
  (17) Diagrams.

/ It is

It is important that training be continuous, whether Battalions or Brigades be in or out of the line.

As there is so much technical knowledge required of all signallers nowadays, to get anything like good communications, it is more important than ever that the men to be trained be selected with great care. Men of intelligence, energy and education are essential.

Battalions should include in the men to be trained a proportion of N.C.Os or men who are likely to become N.C.Os.

<u>Artillery Units.</u>   4.   Exactly the same procedure will be carried out in the case of artillery units. A School will be started near Divl H.Q. under an Officer of the Div. Signal Coy, where artillery signallers who have reached the standard laid down in para (2) will be sent.

The numbers will be 6 from each Artillery Brigade.

..................................Captain.
COMMANDING 41st DIV. SIG. COY. R.E.

27/10/16

41st Div. Signal Coy.
R.E.

War Diary
for
November 1916.

Army Form C. 2118

WAR DIARY
or
INTELLIGENCE SUMMARY
(Erase heading not required.)

Instructions regarding War Diaries and Intelligence Summaries are contained in F. S. Regs., Part II. and the Staff Manual respectively. Title Pages will be prepared in manuscript.

Place	Date	Hour	Summary of Events and Information	Remarks and references to Appendices
RENINGHELST	1/11/16		No change -	
	3/11/16		123 Bde relieve 122 Bde in the left subsector	
	7/11/16		With the recent very heavy rain, the dugouts at the various tent points are getting flooded and much pumping has to be done -	
	8/11/16		One off. 9 Ranks in the Tunnel dugout near N 6 Central which is a Battalion H.Q. Signal Office has to be abandoned. Terminal boards are under water -	
	9/11/16		The 122 Bde relieved 123 Bde in left subsector yesterday - Bde. Signals also relieve -	
	13/11/16		The 4/1st D.A. having rejoined the division from the SOMME area took over from the 1/2nd D.A. at 10 a.m. -	
	16/11/16		The 123 Bde relieve 122 Bde in left subsector -	

Army Form C. 2118

WAR DIARY
or
INTELLIGENCE SUMMARY
(Erase heading not required.)

Place	Date	Hour	Summary of Events and Information	Remarks and references to Appendices
RENINGHELST	19/4/16		It has been decided to experiment with French receiving 'phones instead of B.D.3's. These have been drawn from the Cps today & issued on the following scale 2 to each Bn. 6 to each Bde. & to each Battery & to each Art. Group. A proportion of combined magnetos & holder exchanges are issued with them.	
	23/4/16		122nd Bde relieve 123 Bde in the left Subsector.	
	25/4/16		A scheme for training infantry & artillery signallers has been drawn up & the system of training to be carried out is described in attached Appendix marked "A". The difficulty experienced in starting the Schools is lack of accommodation. The 124 Bde started 10 days ago, the 123 Bde. Starts today. The Artillery to be expected to start in about 10 days time.	see Appendix "A"
	26/4/16		Captain R. Elsdale is temporarily detached from this unit to take up the duties of Acting Brigade Major 123 Inf Bde.	
	27/4/16		123 Bde relieve 122 Bde in left Sector.	
	29/4/16		122 Bde: Signal School commenced today.	W. O. Ramsey Muirhead Capt. O.C. 41 Div Signal Coy R.E.

1875 Wt. W593/826 1,000,000 4/15 J.B.C. & A. A.D.S.S./Forms/C. 2118.

Army Form C. 2118

WAR DIARY
or
INTELLIGENCE SUMMARY
(Erase heading not required.)

Place	Date	Hour	Summary of Events and Information	Remarks and references to Appendices
Field			Casualties during month of November 1916.	
	7/11/16.		3 Other Ranks from Base Signal Depot as reinforcements.	
	8/11/16		93794 Spr O'Brien T. 93765 A/Cpl Davidson A. 93826 Spr Carlin J. 93574 Spr Connor J. 93520 Spr Bullock 96343 Cpl Bird C. 93758 Spr Brown L.au. awarded Mily Medals by XV Corps Cmdr.	
	10/11/16		One Other rank evacuated sick.	
	17/11/16		3 Other ranks from Base Signal Depot as reinforcements.	
	20/11/16		1 " " " " " " "	
	22/11/16		93794 A/C Holland A. 93650 Spr Finnimore P. awarded Mily Medals by H Corps Commander.	
	25/11/16		1 Other rank arrived from Base Signal Depot as reinforcement.	
	26/11/16		1 Other rank evacuated sick.	

William Munhead
Captain
OC 4/1 Signal Coy RE.

30/11/16

WAR DIARY
or
INTELLIGENCE SUMMARY
(Erase heading not required.)

41 Signal Coy Army Form C. 2118

Place	Date	Hour	Summary of Events and Information	Remarks and references to Appendices
			Casualties for the Month of December 1916.	
	26/11/16		One O.R. evacuated sick. Coy	
	28/11/16		One O.R. from Base Signal Depot as reinforcement	
	23/12/16		Capt. A.A. Tayer R.E. from Canadian Corps Sigs assumed command of Company. Coy T.W. Oramp - Bronhart No.4441 vacated command of the company - Coy	
	28/11/16		2 O.R. from Base Signal Depôt as reinforcements. Coy	
	15/12/16		1 O.R. evacuated sick. Coy	
	11/12/16		1 O.R. to England for discharge. Coy	
	6/12/16		1 O.R. from Base Signal Depôt as reinforcement. Coy 3 O.R. apptis from Pioneer in Telegraphists Field Line from 1/11/16. Coy	

A.A.Tayer
Captain R.E.
O.C. 41st/April Coy R.E.

41st Signal Coy.

Signals

JHS

Army Form C. 2118

WAR DIARY
or
INTELLIGENCE SUMMARY
(Erase heading not required.)

Place	Date	Hour	Summary of Events and Information	Remarks and references to Appendices
RENINGHELST	1/12/18		There has been considerable discussion about the S.O.S. system in the left Sector. The results of the tests have been very bad — the system up to date has been the Bn. — Coy line is played through to the Bn. — Artillery Group line. The message has to be transmitted at the Group. It has been decided that a new system is to be brought in at once. Each company to have a separate & distinct S.O.S. line to Bn. H.Q. & thence to its covering battery.	
	2/12/18		The 122 Bde relieve 123 Bde in the left sector.	
	3/12/18		A successful raid was carried out by the 124 Inf Bde. The raiding party entered enemy's trenches & kept in communication the whole time with its battalion HQ. For this purpose a small steel drum was made by Mr Carpenter. This was fitted to carry a D.I. was fitted in the flange — pulled on the reel it worked admirably. The cable which	

Army Form C. 2118

WAR DIARY
or
INTELLIGENCE SUMMARY
(Erase heading not required.)

Instructions regarding War Diaries and Intelligence Summaries are contained in F.S. Regs., Part II. and the Staff Manual respectively. Title Pages will be prepared in manuscript.

Place	Date	Hour	Summary of Events and Information	Remarks and references to Appendices
RENINGHELST	4/12/16		Capt R.C. Smith 20th D.L.I. & 2Lt A. Panch and 10th W. Kents, are attached to the company for one week — These Officers are desirous of joining the Signal Service.	App 7
	9/12/16		123 Bde relieve the 122 Bde — in the left sector —	App 7
	12/12/16		A heavy fall of snow for about 3 hours this morning —	App 7
	16/12/16		122 Bde relieve the 123 Bde in the left sector.	App 7
	17/12/16		O.C. Company attended a conference at 2nd Army to discuss question of Divisional schools for training infantry & artillery signallers —	App 7
	20/12/16		123 Bde relieve 122 Bde in the left sector	App 7
	28/12/16		122 Bde " " 123 " " " "	App 7
	29th		nil.	
	31 Dec			

A.J. Guyer Capt R.E.
O.C. 41 Div Sig Coy R.E.

Army Form C. 2118

WAR DIARY
or
INTELLIGENCE SUMMARY

(Erase heading not required.)

41 D Signal Coy

Vol 9

Instructions regarding War Diaries and Intelligence Summaries are contained in F. S. Regs., Part II. and the Staff Manual respectively. Title Pages will be prepared in manuscript.

Place	Date	Hour	Summary of Events and Information	Remarks and references to Appendices
Runnymede	2-1-17		The 123 Bdes relieve the 122 Bdes	
"	9-1-17		The 122 Bdes relieve the 123 Bdes	
"	16-1-17		The 123 Bdes relieve the 122 Bdes	
"	23-1-17		The 122 Bdes relieve the 123 Bdes	
"	29-1-17		The 123 Bdes relieve the 122 Bdes	

M McC
Patrick H R E
OC 41st Div Sig Coy

Army Form C. 2118

WAR DIARY 41ST DIV. SIG. CO.
or
INTELLIGENCE SUMMARY
(Erase heading not required.)

Instructions regarding War Diaries and Intelligence Summaries are contained in F. S. Regs., Part II. and the Staff Manual respectively. Title Pages will be prepared in manuscript.

Place	Date	Hour	Summary of Events and Information	Remarks and references to Appendices
Remplelat	4/2/17		1 & 2 Inf Bdes Relieve 1 & 3 Inf Bdes in M.C.P	
"	11/2/17		1 & 3 Inf Bdes Relieve 1 & 2 Inf Bdes in M.C.P	
"	18/2/17		1 & 2 Inf Bdes Relieve 1 & 3 Inf Bdes in M.C.P	
"	23/2/17		1 & 3 Inf Bdes Relieve 1 & 2 Inf Bdes in M.C.P	
"	28/2/17		1 & 2 Inf Bdes Relieve 1 & 3 Inf Bdes in M.C.P	

AS Topher
Captain,
COMMANDING 41st DIV. SIG. COY. R.E.

Army Form C. 2118

WAR DIARY 41st Div. Sig. Co. R.E.
or
INTELLIGENCE SUMMARY
(Erase heading not required.)

Vol 10

Place	Date	Hour	Summary of Events and Information	Remarks and references to Appendices
Nice	28/1/17		Casualties for the month of January Feby. 1917.	
"	6/2/17		4 O.R. arrived from Base Sig. Depôt.	
"	12/2/17		2/Lt Mitchell W arrived from Second Army Signal Coy.	
"	10/2/17		2/Lt J.C. Cuthbert & 2 O.R. arrived from Canadian Corps Signals	
			1 O.R. evacuated sick. —	

AJ Payne
Captain R.E.
Comdg. 41/D.Sig.Coy.

Vol XI

Confidential

War Diary
of
41st Div. Signal Coy R.E.

For Month of March 1917

Army Form C. 2118

WAR DIARY
or
INTELLIGENCE SUMMARY
(Erase heading not required.)

Instructions regarding War Diaries and Intelligence Summaries are contained in F.S. Regs., Part II. and the Staff Manual respectively. Title Pages will be prepared in manuscript.

Place	Date	Hour	Summary of Events and Information	Remarks and references to Appendices
Rennyhirst	6/3/17		123 Inf Bde Relieve 122 Bde in the left sub sector	WWP
"	12/3/17		122 Inf Bde Relieve 123 Bde in the left sub sector	WWP
"	17/3/17		Diagram of proposed divisional remits for offensive operations 16 x Copies for approval. Copy of diagram attached	WWP
"	18/3/17		123 Inf Bde Relieve 122 Bde in the left sub sector	WWP
"	21/3/17		57 Inf Bde commenced the relief of the 124 Bde in the right sub sector. 124 Inf Bde started advanced report office at Stenwerck 12 noon	WWP
"	22/3/17		57 Inf Bde completed the relief of the 124 Inf Bde in the right sub sector. 124 Inf Bde office at Clytte closed at 12 noon opened at Stenwerck same hour	WWP
"	24/3/17		122 Inf Bde relieve 123 Bde in the left sub sector. Commenced to bury cable between FA and FJ this evening a distance of 600 yds. Working party of 2 officers and 100 OR from the 123 Rde to continue the extension of and 1 thrill WE. A distance of 3000 yds now completed	WWP

1875 Wt. W593/826 1,000,000 4/15 J.B.C. & A. A.D.S.S./Forms/C. 2118.

Army Form C. 2118

WAR DIARY
or
INTELLIGENCE SUMMARY
(Erase heading not required.)

Instructions regarding War Diaries and Intelligence Summaries are contained in F.S. Regs., Part II. and the Staff Manual respectively. Title Pages will be prepared in manuscript.

Place	Date	Hour	Summary of Events and Information	Remarks and references to Appendices
Ringslet	25/3/17		Working party of 2 officers and 200 OR went interring of 2nd Lieut. Mitchell dispatch RE completion. Phone buried between FA and FJ test boxes	
"	26/3/17		Commenced to bring in trunk distance of 150 yds. Working party of 2 officers and 200 OR from the 123 Brit under the supervision of 2nd Lt. Mitchell RE. A distance of 350 yds completed	
	27/3/17		Working party of 2 officers and 200 OR from the 123 Brit bringing in cables between 9 box and EN 11 a distance of 350 yds completed	
	28/3/17		Working party of 2 officers and 200 OR from the 123 Brit bringing cables between 9 box and EN 11 350 yds completed	
	29/3/17		Work on buried cables suspended owing to the fields intervening	
	30/3/17		" " " " "	
	31/3/17		123 Brit relieve the 122 Brit. Working party of 2 officers and 200 OR from the 122 Brit bringing cables between 9 and EN 11 a distance of 350 yds completed	

Army Form C. 2118

WAR DIARY
or
INTELLIGENCE SUMMARY
(Erase heading not required.)

Instructions regarding War Diaries and Intelligence Summaries are contained in F. S. Regs., Part II. and the Staff Manual respectively. Title Pages will be prepared in manuscript.

Place	Date	Hour	Summary of Events and Information	Remarks and references to Appendices
Leninghelst	1/3/17		1 OR. Evacuated to Casualty Clearing Station	
	6/3/17		2/Lt. R.L. Williams and 1 OR left for 10th Divl Signal Coy.	
	7/3/17		1 OR. arrives from Canadian Corps Signal Co	
	"		1 OR. arrives from Base Signal Depôt	
	10/3/17		Capt. R. Elstob transferred to Second Army H.Q. Signal Coy.	
	15/3/17		1 OR. Wounded in action and Evacuated to hospital	
	21/3/17		2 OR. Evacuated to 10-10 Casualty Clg. Stn.	
	22/3/17		1 OR. arrives from Canadian Corps Signal Coy	
	27/3/17		2 OR. arrives from 41st Base Signal Depôt	

W. Moore
Captain R.E.
O.C. 41 Divl Signal Coy

WAR DIARY or INTELLIGENCE SUMMARY

Army Form C. 2118

Signal H.1

Place	Date	Hour	Summary of Events and Information	Remarks and references to Appendices
Pamphlet	1/4/17		2 Officers and two O.R. bringing cable under the supervision of 2nd Lt Mitchell R.E. A distance of 350 yds completed between E Base and E.W.1	W.P
	2/4/17		2 Officers and two O.R. bringing cable under the supervision of 2nd Lt Mitchell R.E. A distance of 300 yds completed and cable led into E.W.1	W.P
	3/4/17		2 Officers and two O.R. bringing cable under the supervision of Lt Mitchell R.E. A distance of 250 yds completed and cable led into E.W.1 and B. Base	W.P
	4/4/17		2 Officers and two O.R. bringing cable under the supervision of Pnrs R.E. A distance of 250 yds completed between B. Base and Res. Bde.	W.P
	6/4/17	7 am	123 Inf Bde relieve the 123 Inf Bde	W.P
	6/4/17		124 Inf Bde relieve the 123 Inf Bde in the Divisional reserve area	W.P
			123 dig Officer opened at Divisionale at 10 am 124 dig Officer opened in Div Reserve area the same time	
	7/4/17		123 Bde dig Officer opened at Pontferme. During relief of Inf Bdes no bringing trunks available	W.P

1875 Wt. W593/826 1,000,000 4/15 J.B.C. & A. A.D.S.S./Forms/C. 2118.

Army Form C. 2118

WAR DIARY
or
INTELLIGENCE SUMMARY
(Erase heading not required.)

Place	Date	Hour	Summary of Events and Information	Remarks and references to Appendices
Bourghelles	7/4/17		2 Officers and 100 OR Engineers establish telephone B tror and Reo Ptes wiring the supervision of Lieut. Purdie RE. 150 yds completed.	MR
"	8/4/17		A first trunk in telegraphic and telephone communications forward of Bn Hdy and Baty front Hy for testing all direct means of communications Messages were sent and received and the average time good.	MR
	9/4/17		2 Officers and 200 OR Engineers establish telephone B tror and Reo Ptes wiring the supervision of Lieut. Purdie RE. A distance of 300 yds completed.	MR
	10/4/17		2 Officers and 100 OR Engineers cables between B tror and Reo Ptes wiring the supervision of Lieut. Purdie RE. A distance of 275 yds completed. The 122 Inf Bde relieved in the left Battalion sub sector by 140 Inf Bde 47 Div	MR
	11/4/17		2 Officers and 200 OR Engineers cables between B Porce and Reo Ptes wiring the supervision of Lieut. Purdie RE a division B 250 yds completed and completing the work between B Pros and Reo Ptes. 4 Officers and 200 OR Engineers cables between Reo Ptes and Rt Ptes also Rt Ptes and Reo Haven under the supervision of Lieut Purdie RE the work was completed between Reo Ptes and Rt Ptes and 150 yds completed between Rt Ptes and Reo Haven	MR

WAR DIARY
or
INTELLIGENCE SUMMARY
(Erase heading not required.)

Army Form C. 2118

Place	Date	Hour	Summary of Events and Information	Remarks and references to Appendices
Beuvry	12/7/17		Burying cable between RT.Bde and Bois House to Officers and 200 OR under the supervision of Lieut Parsons RE. a distance of 250 yds completed	WP
	13/7/17		4 Officers and 200 OR burying cables between RT.Bde and Bois House under the supervision of Lieut Parsons RE. The cables were nearly completing them	WP
	14/7/17		124 Inf Bde Relieve the 122 Inf Bde in the line	Div
			4 Officers and 200 OR burying cable between Bois House and under the supervision of Lieut Parsons RE a distance of 225 yds completed	WP
	15/7/17		4 Officers and 200 OR burying cable under the supervision of Lieut Parsons RE. a distance of 225 yds completed	WP
	16/7/17		4 Officers and 200 OR burying cables under the supervision of Lieut Parsons RE. a distance of 200 yds completed	WP
	17/7/17		4 Officers and 200 OR burying cable under the supervision of Lieut Parsons RE. a distance of 225 yds completed	WP
	18/7/17		4 Officers and 200 OR burying cables under the supervision of Lieut Parsons a distance of 150 yds completed. This completes burying between Bois House and Bois Forward Posts.	WP

WAR DIARY
or
INTELLIGENCE SUMMARY
(Erase heading not required.)

Army Form C. 2118

Place	Date	Hour	Summary of Events and Information	Remarks and references to Appendices
Rawalpindi	19/4/15		4 Officers and 200 OR laying cables under the supervision of Lieut. Pinnis a division of 250 yds completed between Right and Left R.E.	M.P
"	20/4/17		The 122 Inf Bde relieved the 124 Inf Bde in the line	M.P
	21/4/17		4 Officers and 200 OR laying cables under the supervision of Lieut. Pinnis RE a division of 250 yds completed between Right and Left Bde	M.P
	22/4/17		4 Officers and 200 OR laying cables between Right and Left Bde, a division of 275 yds completed	M.P
	23/4/17		4 Officers and 200 OR laying cables between X Bde and Left Bde a division of 250 yds completed	M.P
	24/4/17		4 Officers and 200 OR laying cables between + Bde and Left Bde a division of 250 yds completed	M.P
	25/4/17		4 Officers and 200 OR laying cables between X Bde and Left Bde this was completed. 124 Inf Bde relieves 122 Bde in the line 123 Inf Bde relieves 122 Bde in Divisional reserve area 122 Inf Bde opened Office at Headquarters	M.P

1875 Wt. W593/826 1,000,000 4/15 J.B.C. & A. A.D.S.S./Forms/C. 2118.

Army Form C. 2118

WAR DIARY
or
INTELLIGENCE SUMMARY
(Erase heading not required.)

Instructions regarding War Diaries and Intelligence Summaries are contained in F. S. Regs., Part II. and the Staff Manual respectively. Title Pages will be prepared in manuscript.

Place	Date	Hour	Summary of Events and Information	Remarks and references to Appendices
Rougefelot	26/7/17		4 Officers and 200 OR bringing cables between Left Bde and Echrus 8 a distance of 250 yds Completed	WP
	27/7/17		4 Officers and 200 OR bringing cables between Left Bde and Echrus 8 a section of roughly completed 122 Inf Bde closed office at Dinanwerk and opened office at Roulepenne at 3pm	WP
	28/7/17		4 Officers and 300 OR bringing cables between Left Bde and Echrus No 8 this was completed	WP
	29/7/17		4 Officers and 200 OR bringing cables between D Bore and E Bore this was completed 122 Inf Bde closed office at Roulepenne and opened office in the Reques area at 4 pm	WP
	30/7/17		4 Officers and 200 OR bringing down wires	WP

Asperine
Major Signals
Comdg Signals et Div

1875 Wt. W593/826 1,000,000 4/15 J.B.C. & A. A.D.S.S./Forms/C.2118.

Army Form C. 2118

WAR DIARY
or
INTELLIGENCE SUMMARY

Chavillir during April 1917.

(Erase heading not required.)

Instructions regarding War Diaries and Intelligence Summaries are contained in F. S. Regs., Part II. and the Staff Manual respectively. Title Pages will be prepared in manuscript.

Place	Date	Hour	Summary of Events and Information	Remarks and references to Appendices
	1.4.17	1.0 p.	arrived from Base Signal Depot	
	3.4.17	1.0 p.	evacuated to Sec. E. Div.	
	12.4.17	1.0 p.	Arrived from Base Signal Depot	
	16.4.17	2.0 p.	Arrived from Base Signal Depot	
	25.4.17	1.0 p.	arrived from Base Signal Depot	
	18.4.17	3.0 p.	Transferred from 1st Div. Sig. Regt.	

30/4/17.

[signature]
Major R.E.
O.C. 4th Div. Signal Co. R.E.

WAR DIARY
or
INTELLIGENCE SUMMARY

Army Form C. 2118

Place	Date	Hour	Summary of Events and Information	Remarks and references to Appendices
Rumanghat	14/5/17		1.2.3 Inf Bde relieve the 1.2.4 Inf Bde on the line	W/P
"	18/5/17		1.2.2 Inf Bde relieve the 1.2.4 Inf Bde on the Div reserve area Rumghat	W/P
			1.2.4 Inf Bde proceed Hotopa to the Gonopilli training area	W/P
			1.2.2 Inf Bde relieve the 1.2.3 Inf Bde on the line	W/P
	21/5/17		Commenced work on a divisional cable route from Div report centre at H.26.A.8.4/2 - 8.b.5 Div Hqrs at Rat Rupilutipa	W/P
	22/5/17			W/P
	23/5/17		1.2.3 Inf Bde relieve the 1.2.2 Inf Bde on the line it. A great deal of work was done during the month burial cables laid into the deep dug outs and front on the Line. There has been an extensive wet very well in view of the fact that they have had an immense amount of rain on us. There are being filled by a working party of 4 O R who are kept constantly employed. We had two of our hutments dry shall too very badly damaged on we have been able to retain on the spot built the other is beyond land repair	W/P

Osborne R.E
Major
COMMANDING 41st DIV. SIG. COY. R.E.

41

WAR DIARY
or
INTELLIGENCE SUMMARY.
(Erase heading not required.)

Signals Vol 13

Army Form C. 2118.

Place	Date	Hour	Summary of Events and Information	Remarks and references to Appendices
Reninghelst	28/6		S.O.R. arrived from Floods Signal Coy	
"	2/7	1.0.	Evacuated to Cinq Rues Base Signal Depot	
"	5/7	1.0.	Arrived from Base Signal Depot	
"	11/7	1.0.	Arrived from Base Signal Depot	
"	14/7	1.0.	Arrived from Base Signal Depot	
"	16/7	1.0.	To Base enroute to Divis'l Wireless to Wireless work	
"	19/7	1.0.	Arrived from 2nd Army Signal Coy	
"	19/7	1.0.	Evacuated to No 50 Gen Clearing Station	

Ustinque
Major RE
O.C. 41 Div Signal Co 88.

WAR DIARY
or
INTELLIGENCE SUMMARY.
(Erase heading not required.)

Army Form C. 2118.

Place	Date	Hour	Summary of Events and Information	Remarks and references to Appendices
BERTHEN	29/5/17		1 O.r. arrived from Base Signal Depot	A1
	1/6/17		1 O.r. Evacuated to No.17 CCS	A2
	3/6/17		1 O.r. Evacuated to No.10 CCS	A3
	4/6/17		1 O.r. Evacuated to No.17 CCS	A4
	7/6/17		1 O.r. Evacuated 6 CCS	A5
			3 O.r. Wounded in action	A6
	12/6/17		1 O.r. arrived from Base Signal Depot	A7
	20/6/17		1 O.r. wounded in action	A8
	21/6/17		1 O.r. wounded in action	A9
	25/6/17		6 O.r. arrived from Base Signal Depot	A10
	27/6/17		2 O.r. arrived from Base Signal Depot	A11
	28/6/17		93784 Cpl McIntyre D.F.	
			93794 L/Cpl Bagnall W.	Awarded the Military Medal by the Field Marshal Commanding-in-Chief
			93760 Spr Clark J.	A12
			93504 Spr Robertson J.	A13

WAR DIARY
or
INTELLIGENCE SUMMARY.

(Erase heading not required.)

Army Form C. 2118.

Place	Date	Hour	Summary of Events and Information	Remarks and references to Appendices
Westoutre	27/6/17	5 pm	Div HQ opened - having moved back from Reningelst (Aug)	
Berthen	30/6/17	9 am	Div HQ opened - Division in rest area (Aug).	

[signatures]

Army Form C. 2118.

WAR DIARY
or
INTELLIGENCE SUMMARY.
(Erase heading not required.)

41ᵗʰ Sig nal Cᵒʸ   Vol 14

Place	Date	Hour	Summary of Events and Information	Remarks and references to Appendices
	29/6/17		93729 Sgt Oxley N.G. ⎫	
			93601 Sgt Hamilton J.C. ⎬ Awarded the Military Medal by the Army	
			93684 Sgt McCulloch H. ⎭ Corps Commander	
			70107 2nd Lieut Dare A.J.	

Army Form C. 2118.

4th April

Vol 13

WAR DIARY
or
INTELLIGENCE SUMMARY.
(Erase heading not required.)

Place	Date	Hour	Summary of Events and Information	Remarks and references to Appendices
Buxton	1/7		The Company moved from WEST to OTR for Trg. — 20 OR of 123 Inf. Bde & 32 OR. of the Dork Observation Detsn have been attached to the Coy for training in Visual Signalling and line work.	
"	2/7		Training as above commenced. Classes of instruction as follows have also been started. (a) Tres. in Telephones & Buzzer working for 3 men from each Inf. Bn Section. (b) Sets for Signallers of R.F.A. 4th Intructions. & (C) Cable Wagon work for 15 OR (Reinforcements) of the Company.	
"	4/7		Major S.N.E. Hitchins Duke of Wellington's Regt. assumed Command of the Company vice Maj. A.A. Payn, P to England for instructional duties.	
"	9/7		Wireless personnel have been transferred to the Company from Wireless Section in view up to strength compared with its equipment. R.A. personnel have been transferred thus completing our R.A. Instruction	

Army Form C. 2118.

WAR DIARY
or
INTELLIGENCE SUMMARY.
(Erase heading not required.)

Instructions regarding War Diaries and Intelligence Summaries are contained in F. S. Regs., Part II. and the Staff Manual respectively. Title pages will be prepared in manuscript.

Place	Date	Hour	Summary of Events and Information	Remarks and references to Appendices
Berthen	14/7		10 O.R. have joined I Corps Signal School for a Learners Course.	
"	17/7		11 O.R. have joined Second Army Signal School for a Learners Course.	
"	20/7		13 O.R. have attended a course of instruction in Wireless at Corps Wireless School.	
"	23/7		Capt Rhoades left for Wireless School by m/c to attend a 5 weeks instructional course. 2 O.R. & 1 Dr. Steps on M.B. 25. R. Relieved in next area by 4 + 7 Divn Sigs	
Berthen	25/7		Relieved 4th & 7th Divn in the line. Lived close to ovens there.	
Westouter	25/7		Signal Office at 3 P.M. Battery Groups were given close to Bluff and Battleworth Groups tactfully signs	
"	26/7		X Corps by motor cars which had arrived — allotted to their stations. Wealowin and F.C's a blend of 13 Amvox Groups Co funwires 16 Btn and Groups were suffering as being experienced in falling lines owing to the H.A. ergo artillery engagement of the Germans at frequent times which be carried in some direction Nost	
		11-30 pm	established German wire line to Bluff Group RFA	

WAR DIARY
or
INTELLIGENCE SUMMARY.
(Erase heading not required.)

Army Form C. 2118.

Instructions regarding War Diaries and Intelligence Summaries are contained in F. S. Regs., Part II, and the Staff Manual respectively. Title pages will be prepared in manuscript.

Place	Date	Hour	Summary of Events and Information	Remarks and references to Appendices
Nedonshi	27/7		Arranged Telephones on all R.F.A. lines to Group's from this Hrs. with unequal and even the same on the telephone exchange to	
"	28/7/17		Neconpai transferred loft 5.30 from established communication with Neconpai transferred. Post through received telephone trunk east of line of Pks in the line	
	29/7/17 30/7/17		Communications have been found to all units. Established communication with W. Bde at SL 37.28 6.40 pm we had a ... ... descended 1/6 no ... ... thought there forward Hrs ... at 15.5 center known. Mitchill were seen on the enemy and shell of heavy shilling by the enemy commenced over after ... extended to all worth at 12 midnight	
	31/7/17		The Telegraph Office to Hrs has been very heavy and all Bgs art details with area 15.00 Wireame they were practically no delay on any of our circuits. A Div Wireal station was established	

A6945 Wt.W14422/M1169 35,000 12/16 D.D.&L. Forms/C/2118/14.

Army Form C. 2118.

WAR DIARY
or
INTELLIGENCE SUMMARY.
(*Erase heading not required.*)

Instructions regarding War Diaries and Intelligence Summaries are contained in F. S. Regs., Part II. and the Staff Manual respectively. Title pages will be prepared in manuscript.

Place	Date	Hour	Summary of Events and Information	Remarks and references to Appendices
Neubedi	31/7		on the short beach at 0.th B.8.2 and although under heavy shell fire kept on towards with the two rifle Batts of front left Bre	

Army Form C. 2118.

WAR DIARY
or
INTELLIGENCE SUMMARY.
(Erase heading not required.)

Place	Date	Hour	Summary of Events and Information	Remarks and references to Appendices
BERTHEN	3/7		1 OR wounded & Evacuated	
	4/7		2 OR arrived from Second Army Rest Camp	
	5/7		4 OR " " " " Base Signal Depot	
	8/7		2 OR left for Second Army Signal Co	
	16/7		1 OR arrived from Base Signal Depot	
	20/7		1 OR departed for "X" Corps Signals	
	22/7		1 OR wounded & Evacuated	
	20/7		1 OR admitted to No 15 CCS Sick	
	24/7		3 OR arrived from Base Signal Depot	

Army Form C. 2118.

41 D Signals Vol 16

WAR DIARY
or
INTELLIGENCE SUMMARY.
(Erase heading not required.)

Instructions regarding War Diaries and Intelligence Summaries are contained in F.S. Regs., Part II. and the Staff Manual respectively. Title pages will be prepared in manuscript.

Place	Date	Hour	Summary of Events and Information	Remarks and references to Appendices
Meherchi	1/8/17		All lines continue to work well to all forward stations	
"	4/8/17		The Beirut route on the Shahluck was cut at 4 am this morning under 2nd Lt Mitchell. Line overhead line and the 13th were able to get through to all stations by 7 am	
"	5/8/17		Beirut route on Shahluck repaired and working OK at 3 pm	
"	"		All our lines were through from this date until one thing advance by the 32nd Div on the 13th retained in return in communication	
Meherchi	13/8/17		Office closed at 9 am and moved at Bukhir same time	
Bukhir	13/8/17		Signal Office opened at 9 am from this date till 21st was used to ordinary all telephones wires thereof to the Coy order were also sent out to Bols action officer	

WAR DIARY
or
INTELLIGENCE SUMMARY.
(Erase heading not required.)

Army Form C. 2118.

Place	Date	Hour	Summary of Events and Information	Remarks and references to Appendices
Bethune	15/8/17		Re-instated all reduced stores belonging to Shoemakers also Bethune	
"	21/8/17		Signal offices closed at 12 noon	
Wagnon	21/8/17		Signal offices opened at 12 noon	
"	22/8/17		Commenced laying Dvr construction exchange on Hay.	
"			Runners & Wires also Common maintenance O 3 and supply	
"			Phones and fixed exchanges	
"	27/8/17		Company commenced moving I this Coy is still well wet. Coy is still well wet and Bell also by rails on third weekly concerts. Bee and Bell also by rails on Person Bays and brightifier working	
"			At end Bee a signal school has been formed to train Bellwire operators	

W M Patrick Capt
& Lg
O C H J C H

Army Form C. 2118.

WAR DIARY
or
INTELLIGENCE SUMMARY.
(Erase heading not required.)

Place	Date	Hour	Summary of Events and Information	Remarks and references to Appendices
	26/2/17		1 OR returned from hospital	
	2/3/17		2 OR wounded in action (Gassed) Evacuated	
	6/3/17		1 OR wounded " " Evacuated	
	2/6/17		2 OR evacuated to CCS (sick)	
	6/6/17			
	9/6/17		2 OR arrived from Base Sig depot 9th	
	14/6/17		1 OR left for 2nd Div Signal Coys	
	17/6/17		1 OR to England sick	
	17/7/17		1 OR to Base Signal Depot	
	19/7/17		1 OR transferred to his unit from 27A	
	7/08/17		2 OR awarded the Military Medal by Corps Commdr	

Signal 41 Army Form C. 2118.

Vol / 157

WAR DIARY
or
INTELLIGENCE SUMMARY.
(Erase heading not required.)

Place	Date	Hour	Summary of Events and Information	Remarks and references to Appendices
WIZERNES	1/9/17		Spent in cleaning up instruments, wagons etc. Infantry Signallers finished course and were examined with very satisfactory results.	
	2/9/17		Nothing to report. RA arrived at WIZERNES	RA arrived at WIZERNES
	3/9/17		Div Observation Section course in flag, lamp and helio brought to close owing to their going "up the line" Second course commenced for Bde & Battalion signallers in Power Buzzer and amplifier working. OC and Capt Patrick went to LA CLYTTE and opened up Report Centre there.	HQRA
	4/9/17		Lt Purves reported to AD Signals X Corps with 12 OR for work in forward area.	
	5/9/17		190 Bde RFA moved to STEENVOORDE. OC returned from LA CLYTTE	
LA CLYTTE			Nothing to report	
STEENVOORDE	6/9/17		190 Bde RFA moved from STEENVOORDE to GODWAERSVELDE	Section was being trained in cable & telephone working

Army Form C. 2118.

WAR DIARY
or
INTELLIGENCE SUMMARY.
(Erase heading not required.)

Instructions regarding War Diaries and Intelligence Summaries are contained in F. S. Regs., Part II. and the Staff Manual respectively. Title pages will be prepared in manuscript.

Place	Date	Hour	Summary of Events and Information	Remarks and references to Appendices
WIZERNES	7/9/17		Nothing to report	
	8/9/17		Artillery Hqrs with RA Section moved to RENINGHELST Second course of Div¹ Battalion signallers in Buzz Buzz and amplifier working finished	
	9/9/17		Lt Jefferies went up to YDAR for burying cable in forward area.	
	10/9/17		Practice attack by Division carried out. "Forward Party" working practices and results were excellent. Cable was buried from H30 b 5.7 (Sheet 28 NW4 and NE3) to H30 b 55.40. Great difficulty was experienced owing to small number of working party with shovels (70) & hostile shelling	
	11/9/17		Cable buried forward to H30 b 85.30 and previous nights work well banked up	
	12/9/17		Forward bury well banked up and tested out	
	13/9/17		Nothing to report	

WAR DIARY
or
INTELLIGENCE SUMMARY.
(Erase heading not required.)

Army Form C. 2118.

Place	Date	Hour	Summary of Events and Information	Remarks and references to Appendices
	14/9/17		Company moved to TERDEGHEM arriving 4pm. Billeted here for night	
ZEVECOTEN	15/9/17		Company moved to ZEVECOTEN Arrived about noon. Signal office opened 10am	
	16/9/17		More forward buried work was to have been done, but no working party turned up	
	17/9/17		Buried route carried forward from J30 & 85.30 to J19 c.5.2. 122 Bde moved to HEDGE STREET and D14 to CANADA STREET and took over line.	
	18/9/17		Great difficulty in establishing communication to Bdes owing to trouble on Corps bury.	
	19/9/17		All Inf Bdes and Artillery Groups were got through during the day	
	20/9/17		Division attacked. Communication to Bdes and forward worked very successfully. Outgoing messages 513 Incoming 394 D.R.L.S. 358	

Army Form C. 2118.

WAR DIARY
or
INTELLIGENCE SUMMARY.
(Erase heading not required.)

Place	Date	Hour	Summary of Events and Information	Remarks and references to Appendices
ZEVECOTEN	21/9/17		At 3am RENINGHELST-DICKEBUSCH route was cut badly by shell fire, and all Bde & Group lines were cut. 8 Corps Maintenance Gang was sent for and all lines were through before 9.30am. The division made a further attack at 9.30am. All lines worked well after 9.30am.	
	22/9/17		All lines worked well during day. Division (less Artillery) was relieved during night of 22-23rd by 39th Division.	
ZEVECOTEN & CAESTRE	23/9/17		39th Division took over at 10am. Company moved off to CAESTRE. Lt Mitchell & 10 OR left behind to assist Corps in burying cable.	
CAESTRE	24/9/17		Nothing to report	
	25/9/17		Company transport moved to ZERMEZEELE area and camped for night.	
LA PANNE	26/9/17		Transport Company moved from ZERMEZEELE area to LA PANNE. Company opened office & noon. Remainder of Company moved from CAESTRE to LA PANNE in lorries	

Army Form C. 2118.

WAR DIARY
or
INTELLIGENCE SUMMARY.
(Erase heading not required.)

Instructions regarding War Diaries and Intelligence Summaries are contained in F. S. Regs., Part II. and the Staff Manual respectively. Title pages will be prepared in manuscript.

Place	Date	Hour	Summary of Events and Information	Remarks and references to Appendices
LA PANNE	27/9/17		Nothing to report	
	28/9/17		Nothing to report	
	29/9/17		Nothing to report	
	30/9/17		Nothing to report	

Army Form C. 2118.

WAR DIARY
or
INTELLIGENCE SUMMARY.
(Erase heading not required.)

Instructions regarding War Diaries and Intelligence Summaries are contained in F. S. Regs., Part II. and the Staff Manual respectively. Title pages will be prepared in manuscript.

Place	Date	Hour	Summary of Events and Information	Remarks and references to Appendices
In the Field	27/8		1 OR arrived from Base Signal Depot	
	30/8		1 OR arrived from Casualty Clearing Station	
	31/8		1 OR awarded the Military Medal by Corps Commander for Gallantry in the Field	
			1 OR awarded the D.C.M. by the Corps Commander for Gallantry in the Field	
	2/9		2 ORs arrived from the Base Signal Depot as reinforcements	
	6/9		2 ORs evacuated to MDS	
	6/9		3 ORs arrived from Base Signal Depot as reinforcements	
	20/9		1 OR killed in action & ORs wounded in action	
	24/9		1 OR wounded in action & evacuated to Hospital	
			1 OR arrived from Base Signal Depot	
	25/9		1 OR wounded in action (Gassed) evacuated	
			1 OR evacuated to No. 1 C.C.S.	

Manningford Maj. R.E.
O.C.

41st. Divisional Signal School.

STANDING ORDERS.

(1). TIME TABLE.

      Reveille .... 6.0 am.
      Roll Call................ 6.15 am.
      1st. Parade.............. 7.0 am.
      Breakfast................ 8.0 am.
      Inspection of rooms...... 8.45 am.
      2nd. Parade.............. 9.0 am.
      Dinners.................. 1.0 pm.
      Afternoon Parade......... 2.0 pm.
      Tea...................... 5.0 pm.
      Roll Call................ 8.30 pm.
      Lights out............... 9.0 pm.

(2). DRESS.
    Dress for parades. - S.Dress, Puttees, belt and P.H.Helmet. Caps and belts will not be worn at meals. Buttons and boots will be polished.

(3). Rifles will be inspected daily by squad commanders after afternoon parade.
P.H. Helmets, Box respirators, Rifles, Ammunition and Iron rations will be inspected every Thursday on the 9.0 am parade by the chief instructor.
The 9.0 am parade on Thursdays will be in marching order.

(4). On each Sunday there will be a Church Parade for all ranks. Dress - drill order, without rifles.

(5) Tests on all subjects including a written paper will be carried out on Fridays and Saturdays.

(6). Saturday afternoon will be observed as a holiday for all men who pass their weekly tests. Men who fail in their weekly tests will parade as usual on Saturday afternoon.

(7). Any man who does not make satisfactory progress, or who misbehaves will be at once returned to his unit.

(8). The watch in the Signal Office window is the correct time.

                      (signed) E. N. F. HITCHINS.
                                            Major,
11-9-1917.   O.C., Signals, 41 Division.

WAR DIARY or INTELLIGENCE SUMMARY

Army Form C. 2118.

Place	Date	Hour	Summary of Events and Information	Remarks and references to Appendices
LA PANNE	1/10/17		Three weeks course in Wireless, Power Buzzer and Amplifier working for Bde and Btn Signallers commenced. 42 men attended.	
	2/10/17		Capt Patrick went to COXYDE BAINS to look round communications of 32nd Division	
	3/10/17		Nothing to report	
	4/10/17		Orders came for Division to relieve 42nd Division on the 7th October. Maj Hitchins and Capt Patrick went over to 42nd Division to look over communications.	
	5/10/17		Lt Mitchell returned from duty with 10th Corps	
	6/10/17		Lt Purves returned from leave and took over "Signals" 122 Bde from Lt Sylvestre. Lt Mitchell took over "Signals" 123 Bde. Lt Sylvestre reported for duty at Division. On night of 6/7/17 123 Bde relieved the 127 Inf Bde in the line. Division Signal Coy (less Transport (horse)) moved to	
ST IDESBALDE	7/10/17			

Army Form C. 2118.

WAR DIARY
or
INTELLIGENCE SUMMARY.
(Erase heading not required.)

Place	Date	Hour	Summary of Events and Information	Remarks and references to Appendices
ST. IDESBALDE	7/10/17 (contd)		ST IDESBALDE. Took over from 42nd Division at 10 a.m. 124th Inf Bde relieved 126th Inf Bde in COXYDE BAINS Coast defence Sector. 122 Inf Bde remained at LA PANNE. Communications all OK. in reserve	
	8/10/17		LT STANWORTH reported for duty at Divisional from 123 Inf Bde. Horse lines moved to fresh quarters in LA PANNE.	
	9/10/17		Instructors arrived for Divisional Signal School commencing on 11th. 40 line exchange brought back from Forward Hqrs and installed at DHQ in place of 10 and 20 line boards. 20 line board taken up to replace.	
	10/10/17		Men arrived for Divisional Signal School commencing 11th inst.	
	11/10/17		Signal School spent day in sandbagging huts etc. Kit inspection of School was also held during morning. Wet	
	12/10/17		Canteen opened at School. Artillery took over from 42nd Divnl Artillery at 12 noon. Hdqrs ST. IDESBALDE. Test carried out at School in afternoon.	

WAR DIARY or INTELLIGENCE SUMMARY.

Army Form C. 2118.

Place	Date	Hour	Summary of Events and Information	Remarks and references to Appendices
ST. IDESBALDE	12/10/17		187th Bde RGA took over from 211th Bde RGA on nights 11/12 13/14th	
	13/10/17		School completed sandbagging of huts.	
	14/10/17		Nothing to report	
	15/10/17		122 Inf Bde relieved the 124th Inf Bde in the COXYDE-BAINS Coast Defense Sector. The 124th Inf Bde relieved the 123rd Inf Bde in the NIEUPORT BAINS Sector. 123rd Inf Bde moved to LA PANNE in Dunk Reserve.	
	16/10/17		On the nights 16/17th and 17/18th 190 Bde RGA relieved the 39th Bde RGA. Dunk Hqrs shelled during night	
	17/10/17		DD Signals visited OC Signals and inspected school and Signal office. Signal office fortified with sandbags	
	18/10/17		Nothing to report	
	19/10/17		Lt Mitchell proceeded on leave. Weekly test at Dunk Signal Cross. Results satisfactory	
	20/10/17		Capt Patrick proceeded on leave. Lt Mitchell proceeded on leave	

WAR DIARY
or
INTELLIGENCE SUMMARY.
(Erase heading not required.)

Army Form C. 2118.

Place	Date	Hour	Summary of Events and Information	Remarks and references to Appendices
ST IDESBALD	21/10/17		Nothing to report	
	22/10/17		Left Coy SOS line put through. Right also put through during forenoon, but cable in "J" Trench cut by shell fire during afternoon, caused it to become dis. Area people advised.	
	23/10/17		Considerable trouble caused in communications forward of Arty and Inf. Bdes owing to hostile shellfire. All routes were repaired during day. On night 24/25th 2nd (Army Bde NZFA) were transferred from Right Divn to this Divn and relieved 158 Bde (Army Bde)	
	24/10/17			
	25/10/17		Lt Sylvester went to Army on Gas Course. (Sundays)	
	26/10/17		Cable in "K" and "F" Trenchs cut during day	
	27/10/17		One shell pitched in ST. IDESBALDE during afternoon	
	28/10/17		Division relieved by 9th Division. Relief started. Officers men Lorries Shed	
ST MALO LES BAINS	29/10/17		Division moved to ST MALO LES BAINS with artillery complete. Relief completed. Signal Office opened at 10am	

Army Form C. 2118.

WAR DIARY
or
INTELLIGENCE SUMMARY.
(Erase heading not required.)

Instructions regarding War Diaries and Intelligence Summaries are contained in F. S. Regs., Part II. and the Staff Manual respectively. Title pages will be prepared in manuscript.

Place	Date	Hour	Summary of Events and Information	Remarks and references to Appendices
ST MALO LES BAINS	30/10/17		Nothing to report. Signal School closed on orders by 9th Division. Class returned to their units. Any equipment & getting ready for a distinct move by rail, with a proposed departure at the other end. All ranks received 48 hours leave on 28th inst.	
	31/10/17		Lt Mitchell returned from leave. Capt Patrick returned from leave.	

A6945 Wt.W1422/M1160 358,000 12/16 D.D.&L. Forms/C./2118/14.

WAR DIARY
or
INTELLIGENCE SUMMARY.

Army Form C. 2118.

4th Div Sub Signal Coy

O/C 1/8

Place	Date	Hour	Summary of Events and Information	Remarks and references to Appendices
	28/8/17		1 OR Evacuated to C.C.S.	
	17/9/17		1 OR Evacuated to Casualty Clearing Stn.	
	18/9/17		1 OR Awarded Military Medal by Corps Commdr. for gallantry	
	20/9/17		1 OR " " " " " "	
			1 OR " bar to " " " "	
	9/10/17		3 ORs arrived from Base Signal Depot	
	28/10/17		1 OR " " " " "	
	31/10/17		1 OR " " 39th Div. Signal Coy RE	
			1 OR Evacuated to CCS	

41st Div.
G. 458.
34/20.

122nd Infantry Brigade.
123rd Infantry Brigade.
124th Infantry Brigade.
C. R. A.
Camp Commandant.
" Q ".
41st Divl. Signal Coy.

DIVISIONAL SIGNAL SCHOOL.

1.- The Divisional Wireless School and the Brigade and Battalion Signal Schools will be absorbed into a Divisional Signal School from the 11th inst.

2.- The O.C. 41st Divl. Signal Coy. will be Commandant of the Divisional Signal School, and he will appoint an officer of 41st Divl. Signal Coy. to act as Chief Instructor.

3.- The Signal School will be situated at Divisional Headquarters.

4.- Each Infantry Brigade will provide 5 N.C.O. Assistant Instructors, one of these to be from the Brigade Signal Section. These N.C.O's will be selected from the N.C.O's at present instructing at the Brigade and Battalion Signal Schools.
The above to report to O.C. 41st Divl. Signal Coy. at Divisional Headquarters at 9 a.m. on 9th October.
Each Brigade R.F.A. will provide one N.C.O. Assistant Instructor who will report at same place and time.
Each Infantry Brigade will also provide one man to act as cook and two men as fatigue men to report at same place and time.

5.- The following courses will start at ST. IDESBALD at 9 a.m. 11th October, 1917 :-

    (a) The Wireless Course as at present assembled.
    (b) Course for partially trained men (i.e. from the existing Brigade Sections), 24 Other Ranks from each Infantry Brigade. Total 72.
    (c) Course for beginners :-
        60 Other Ranks from each Infantry Brigade, and
        20 Other Ranks from each Artillery Brigade. Total 220.

The above will report to O.C. Signals, 41st Division, at Divisional Headquarters at 5 p.m. on the 10th October, 1917. They will be fully equipped and each man will bring with him one signalling flag, two days rations, and blanket.

6.- Battalions will continue to train Signallers at present under instruction, less those sent to the Divisional Signal School. These Signallers will be selected for course (b) at the Divisional Signal School, as soon as they can pass a test at 4 words per minute on visual instruments and six words per minute on the buzzer.

7.- Men will be returned to their units when they can pass a test as first class signallers.

8.- Units who wish to send officers to either (a), (b) or (c) courses will apply direct to O.C. 41st Divl. Signal Coy.

9.- The following equipment will be provided by each Infantry Brigade :-

       3 Lucas Lamps.
       6 D.III Telephones.
       6 Signalling Shutters.

The above stores will be sent to O.C. 41st Divl. Signal Coy. at 9 a.m. on the 9th inst.

10.- Nominal rolls of men attending (b) and (c) Courses will be forwarded to O.C. Signals, 41st Division, by 6 p.m. 9th October.

5th October, 1917.   Lt. Colonel. G.S.

Army Form C. 2118.

41 D Signal [Vol 14]

WAR DIARY
or
INTELLIGENCE SUMMARY.
(Erase heading not required.)

Place	Date	Hour	Summary of Events and Information	Remarks and references to Appendices
St Idesbalde	27/10/17		1 OR to England for trade course	
MALO	31/10/17		1 OR arrived from 39th Div Signal Coy R.E.	
	1/11/17		1 OR Evacuated to No 15 C.C.S. (sick)	
			1 OR arrived from the Army Troops Supply Column	
			1 OR transferred to " " " "	
	29/9/17		1 OR admitted to hospital whilst on leave to UK 20/9/17 to 20/10/17	
	18/11/17		1 OR evacuated to No 66 F. Amb. sick	
	21/11/17		1 OR " " " "	
	29/11/17		1 OR " " " "	

1st Signal Coy Order No 5
22 Nov 1917

I. The British force will move towards MONTE BALUNA to support the Italian Army.

II. The Headquarters of this No 1 Signal Company under Captn Patrick RE will march at 9 am & will pass starting point SPESSA at 11.15 am

Destination: ALBETTONE
Route BAGNOLO – SPESSA –
ORGIANO – COLLEREDO –
CAMPIGLIA

III. No 1 B Cable detachment will march at 7 am under orders of Lt Sylvester

IV. No 1 A Cable detachment will move at 11.30 by Bus and will be relieved by them from Dr. Austen

HSS 201   23.11.17

St Sylvester.

(I) You will march with your detachment at 7 a.m. tomorrow to ALBETTONE. Route BAGNOLO – SPESSA – TRONCIO – COLEREDO – CAMPIGLIA

(II) From the divisional signal office at ALBETTONE you will lay a line to PONTE DI COSTOZZA, leaving a drop office at PONTE DI BARBARANO.

(III) The line will be through by 5 PM, at which hour Brigades will send orderlies to the wagon office & drop office and communication will be open.

(IV) B Cable wagon with an empty drum will be left at ALBETTONE

(IV) and will reel up the line when the Division moves on 25th inst.

(V) You will arrange billets for your detachments at PONTE DI BARBARANO and PONTE DI COSTOZZA. Rations for 24th inst will be carried.

VJMcKenna?
Major

1152/2

Lt Jefferies

You will march tomorrow under orders of 122 Inf Bde who will ration you from evening/night of 24th inst.

Report to BM 122 Inf Bde for orders.

You will probably be required to lay cable on 25th inst.

EM Williams
Maj

23.11.17

(I) Dropped... [illegible handwritten notes]
... CAMP DIED in a
... VILLA DEL CONTE
Route VILLANOVA - DOMENE b
- CAMPO S. MARTINO - BUSA AT
Distance 19½ miles

(II) Linked... across the
river BRENTA at CURTAROLO
Bridge

(III) A Chalk... with
... the company at
Villa Del Conte returned

(IV) ... Parade 6.30 am
[illegible signature]

MSS 204

41 Div Second Corps ?
Aug 6   24 + 17

I. The advance will be
continued to-morrow.
Destination CAMPANA &
ROUTE MONTECCHIA — ......
March off at 7.30 a.m.
....
.... GAS MASKS

II. B. will .... , I Cadre ...
will man .... bay ...
... with the ....
PTE della STAZZA
These ....
... attack
Route SECULA — P ....
L.G. Tirol 6 ag CRISTO VACO —
BARONA — ......

(iii) A Wagon, 1 B ....
... not ... & C ....
+ 1 pick 2 / & CAMP ...
hydraulic trailer on ... ...
from SECULA

HSS 210

41st Signal Coy
Order No 8

I. The march will be resumed tomorrow

II. Destination:- LEVADA & Kil SW of BEDOERC

III. Route:- Last E of VILLA DEL CONTE - CAMPSANPIERO - BUSTICO - S TIZIANO - X Rds W of TREBASELEGHE - MARCANTON

IV. Time of starting 9-20 AM
Head of Coy to pass X Rds Half mile E of VILLA DEL CONTE 9-45 AM, and to pass road junction at S TIZIANO at 1-50 PM in rear of 122 Inf Bde

V. Coy Drawn up in order of Route on main Road outside Billets ready to march at 9-15 AM

V   1st Parade 6-30 am

VI Div Hd Qrs will close at VILLA DEL
    CONTE & reopen at LEVADA at
    12 NOON 28 Inst

27-11-17   EMHitchens
                        Major
                        So'bted
                OC 41st Div Signal Co RE

www.ingramcontent.com/pod-product-compliance
Lightning Source LLC
Chambersburg PA
CBHW081532160426
43191CB00011B/1742